SITTINGBOURNE
A History

Sittingbourne's railway station in the early days, c.*1909.*

SITTINGBOURNE
A History

John Clancy

Phillimore

2007

Published by
PHILLIMORE & CO. LTD
Madam Green Farm, Chichester, West Sussex, PO20 2DD, England
www.phillimore.co.uk

© John Clancy, 2007

ISBN 978-1-86077-462-1

Printed and bound in Great Britain

Contents

List of Illustrations

Frontispiece: Sittingbourne's railway station in the early days, *c.*1909.

Acknowledgements

I would like to record my sincerest thanks and gratitude to the following people for all their help and assistance in compiling this book. Without them it would not have been possible to present a full and accurate picture of the origins and history of Sittingbourne: Alan Abbey, Barry Kinnersley, Bryan Clark, David Harvey, *East Kent Gazette*, Brian Turner, Fred Atkins, Mick Clancy, *Local History Publications*, David Colthup, the Faversham Society, the Sittingbourne Society, Mr F. Littlewood, Chris Deamer, Alan Cordell, the *Cambria* Trust, Sittingbourne Heritage Museum, Mike Smith, Robert Dixon of *George Webb Finn*, Phil Talbot.

Finally, acknowledgement has to be made to the work of early postcard photographers like Ferris, Ramell, Wrigglesworth, Shrubshall, Ash *et al*, without whom we would not have early views of our town. Many of their scenes have not changed much in a century or more. Only close inspection reveals the many subtle changes.

While every effort has been made to authenticate all the information received from these people and other sources, time can sometimes play tricks on the memory so if any part of my text is inaccurate I sincerely apologise and will endeavour to correct it in any future editions of this book. Every reasonable effort has been made to contact the copyright holders of the photos and illustrations used herein but should there be any errors or omissions or people whom I could not contact, I will be pleased to insert the appropriate acknowledgement in any future edition.

JOHN CLANCY

Introduction

'*Another* book on the history of Sittingbourne?' you ask. 'What more can be told about the town?' It has been suggested that every generation rewrites history and the perceived past is merely a pale reflection of the present. In the past 30 years the interval between rewriting has been reduced from a generation to periods often as short as only a few months. New information comes to light all the time and the study of local history can be likened to completing a jigsaw puzzle in which, piece by piece, the overall picture finally emerges. With the passing of time comes the opportunity to refine theories and hypotheses as new facts present themselves. The history of any town can be approached from at least four different angles (documentary evidence, historical geography, place-name evidence and archaeology), each of which has developed rapidly over the past few years, but the process has been speeded up and made more complex by the interplay between these different disciplines. It is only when these four approaches are pooled together that a concise history of any town can be told. This book differs from previously published works in that it concentrates on Sittingbourne alone and does not include neighbouring Milton Regis and Murston, apart from the occasional necessary reference. This allows more space to be devoted to aspects of the town's past that have never been covered before.

Sittingbourne is a ribbon development town on the Roman road Watling Street, now designated the A2, 40 miles east of London and approximately the same distance from Dover; it is roughly equidistant between the cathedral cities of Rochester and Canterbury. It is due to this unique position that the town came to prominence. Watling Street has long been Britain's main artery for communication with the continent, giving Kent a position of national importance. It augmented the natural waterways and coastal routes of the region, fostering growth in the surrounding parishes, so Sittingbourne's location on the Thames and Medway estuaries with their creeks and navigable rivers was at least as important in regard to the transport of goods and our long-term economic stability. Sittingbourne sits on the southern bank of Milton Creek, the estuary of several small streams that once flowed from the Downlands to the south. Our golden age was during the medieval pilgrimages when the town earned a reputation for the quality of its hospitality, but their decline following the Reformation reduced the traffic flow along Watling Street, adversely affecting the economy of those towns for which hospitality was a principal feature.

Sittingbourne's history goes back a thousand years and more; its residents have been building and rebuilding on the original burgage plots ever since. New construction technologies, changing architectural fashions and fluctuations in the local socio-economic dynamic have each had their effects over the years and it is now difficult to visualise just how the town might have once looked. It would have been far smaller than it is today, stretching from the parish church westwards along

1 *Hasted's c.1798 map of Sittingbourne, showing it to be a ribbon development along Watling Street. It highlights the manors that surrounded the town and the agrarian nature of the countryside. [Picture courtesy of* Local History Publications]

London and became an access route to the network of waterways and ports that could carry goods more efficiently. As the quantity of goods increased, so too did the number of vessels used to transport them, something road traffic could not compete with. Towns like Milton and Faversham prospered. It is recorded that, for example, of all the corn shipments sent to London in 1650, Milton sent as much as the larger ports of Rochester and Maidstone combined. Being a very small port Sittingbourne could not accommodate the new, larger vessels commerce of the period required. The town's population had by now risen to 300 with 88 inhabited houses stretching roughly from West Lane to Central Avenue.

The town has never been known for the beauty or quality of its architecture but in general its more impressive buildings, once occupied by its wealthier citizens, are located on the south side of the High Street. The High Street might have become more attractive had it not been for the Georgian buildings being spoilt by the later addition of unsympathetic modern shopfronts. A few do survive and for that we must be grateful.

Many aspects of the town's history justify a separate book being devoted to themselves and in some cases, like brick-making, paper-making and barge-building, such books have already been published. This book is intended to be a general comprehensive history of the town so it is not possible for any particular aspect to be covered in detail. It is my intention to guide you through the general history of the town, beginning with an overview of where the original inhabitants might have come from and who they were, to the early days of medieval Sittingbourne when the town began to develop, to our prosperous period of industrial development, urban

the modern High Street towards Central Avenue but there is the suggestion it also spread along East Street as evidenced by the age of certain buildings there.

In the 17th century the continuing rise in London's population called for more food and goods to be sent from Kent. As the need for efficient and cost-effective transport increased, those towns that made a living from their position on the coast and creeks grew in stature. The socio-economic focus of Kent shifted from the earlier industrial Weald to north Kent where the population steadily began to increase, despite the unhealthy environment of the marshes. The region rapidly became an important link for most of Kent's commercial enterprises with the capital. At about this time Watling Street stopped being just a through-road from Dover to

2 *Aerial view of the western end of town from the 1920s.*

3 *Aerial view of the central part of town from the 1920s.*

growth and civic developments in the 20th and 21st centuries. Over a period of almost a thousand years the focus of the town has moved from it being a medieval centre of hospitality to a 19th-century industrial centre to what it is today, a role that's difficult to define. Several of the town's original inns, notably the *Red Lion* and the *George*, can still be seen, while others, like the *Rose*, have become concealed behind modern shop fronts. All traces of the 19th- and 20th-century brick fields have been wiped from the landscape. The creek that shaped the original settlement is now but a shadow of its former self, the streams that once flowed into it have all dried up and the barge and shipbuilding yards that once lined its banks have long gone. Sittingbourne today is a very different place to what it once was. Since amalgamating with Milton and Murston in the 1920s it has grown from a small hamlet to a large conurbation that is part of the civic administrative district of northern Kent known as Swale, a name taken from the stretch of water that separates the Isle of Sheppey from the mainland.

Chapter 1

The Origins of the Town

Sittingbourne was once so small and insignificant it did not even warrant a mention in Domesday Book. It was actually a part of Milton Regis, an economically and socially more important town that was an ancient royal demesne. A conservation study undertaken by the Kent County Council in 1974 inferred, 'This locality in North Kent has been used for settlement or burial at least since Roman times, but Sittingbourne and Milton Regis are places about which little is widely known, perhaps because they have not seemingly played an important part in the religious or political events in Kentish history.' The town's trade directory of 1908 maintained, 'Sittingbourne's history is unknown until medieval times when there was a continuous stream of pilgrims passing through to the shrine of St Thomas á Becket at Canterbury.' This was when the town started to develop and grow as a separate entity, a time when many locals will tell you the town 'began', but what about its early roots? Where did the original settlers come from? From what did the town's innkeeping economy evolve?

Before the Norman Conquest the area known as Milton Hundred was centred on the town and manor of Milton, or Middletun, an administrative district in the Jutish kingdom of Kent which was divided into administrative areas known as Lathes. There were five full Lathes and two Half-Lathes; Milton was one of the latter and was exceptional in that whereas the other Lathes were sub-divided into Hundreds, smaller administrative areas, Milton was

also Milton Hundred. It could well be that this unusual situation was a reflection of Milton's wealth and royal connections. Milton was the centre for local trade and commerce for the whole Hundred and Manor of Milton and Marden, which included 18 parishes from Rainham in the west to Tonge in the east, Milsted to the south and Iwade to the north; it also included the Isle of Sheppey except for Harty, which belonged to Faversham and the Wealden village of Marden, covering an area of some 17,000 acres. According to the lay subsidy of 1334–5 north-east Kent, of which Sittingbourne was a part, was assessed as being worth over 20 shillings per square mile, the largest area to be assessed at this level in south-east England and was one of the highest levels in the country. It has often been said the origins and history of any town, city or village are encapsulated in its name. If this is so, what is the meaning of 'Sittingbourne'? In their 1960s town guide the urban district council suggested the town's name simply derived from a Saxon clan, the 'Sydingas' who settled here around a 'bourne' or stream. Our interpretation has moved on considerably in the intervening 40 years and there are now several possibilities to consider, each an intriguing and interesting hypothesis, but none of which can be fully substantiated. The name almost certainly originated in Anglo-Saxon times when it was spelt 'Saedingaburne', which, according to Judith Glover in her book *The Place Names of Kent*, translates as 'the stream of the slope dwellers'. This is endorsed by the *Oxford Dictionary of Placenames*,

4 *The Court Hall, Milton Regis, the civic centre of the Hundred of Milton since the 16th century when the hall was built. This building acted as the manorial centre, court house and town gaol. [Barry Kinnersley]*

which spells the word as 'Sidingeburn' and dates it as such to A.D. 1200. It has been inferred that the name derived from the Saxon word 'saething', meaning a seething or babbling brook, a theory taken up in the history book of Watling Street, *The Old Dover Road*. The original settlement might have been situated on the slope overlooking the stream that once flowed down what is now Bell Road and Crown Quay Lane but it is doubtful whether the original settlement stood anywhere near where modern Sittingbourne is now situated; it was more likely to have stood slightly to the north on the bank of the creek where the town's two quays, Crown Quay and Holdredge, later developed.

'Sedingbourne', or 'Saedingburga' as it was spelt by the Anglo-Saxons, is said to translate as 'the hamlet beside the creek', an interpretation that might be somewhere near the truth as it describes the original settlement's conjectured location perfectly. The Saxons' reference to 'Sidyngbourn' can be found in Saxon documents dated A.D. 989 as well as in contemporary records of the 13th and 14th centuries.

By the late 15th and early 16th centuries there were two different spellings, 'Sydingborn' and 'Sythingborn', but, as illiteracy was both widespread and common, the name could easily have been mis-spelt. Another suggestion is that the town's name stemmed from this being an area of land occupied by a tribe called Sything or Syding; some spellings are written as 'Sydingasborn' or 'Sythingasborn', which makes more sense. The 'ingas' element of the name derives from the Jutish word meaning 'at the place of' or 'belonging to'. A 'born' is obviously a bourne or stream so it must be assumed the first element, 'Syd' or 'Syth', was either the tribe or its leader. However, whereas this hypothesis can be applied to Sittingbourne, Bobbing, Eastling, Detling, Malling *et al*, it should be regarded with a degree of caution; not all place names that contain or end in '-ing' were originally '-ingas' names. Garlinge and Sandling for example contain the Old English element 'hlinc', which means 'a bank'; hence the place names equate to 'green bank' and 'sand bank' respectively. When Canon Scott Robertson wrote his history of Sittingbourne in 1879 he suggested the town's name was more commonly written as 'Sedyngburne', maintaining that the first part of the word alludes to the tribal name of those who lived here, the Soedingas, but evidence of such a tribe is slim. Unfortunately the exact meaning of the town's name has been lost with the passing of time, so all we are left with is assumption and conjecture.

There seems to be little doubt that the town had its origins in the Anglo-Saxon period when 'Seda' or 'Ceda' was a common enough name element, but prior to that there could well have been an unnamed settlement here. There is one other explanation that should be taken with the proverbial pinch of salt, a quaint local tale that suggests the town took its name from the passing pilgrims who were often seen 'sitting by the bourne', presumably soaking their aching feet, but this is just a local myth. If there was any truth in this tale, by what name was the settlement known before the pilgrimages began, because without any shadow of doubt one did exist? [See Note 1]

Before investigating the origins of Sittingbourne it would be useful to look firstly at the early occupation of the area in general. Two thousand years ago much of the land to the north of the present A2 road was marshland, an environment not really suitable for habitation, but it is known that settlements existed at Milton, Murston and Tonge where the residents 'suffered from the ague'. In 1688 a certain Dr Plot observed that seldom did anyone who lived on the banks of the creek live much beyond the age of twenty-one. This led Will Lambarde to write in his *Perambulations of Kent* in 1570, 'He that will not live long, let him live in Murston, Teynham or Tonge.' In his *History of Kent,* published in 1828, W.H. Ireland reported how the air around the creek was impregnated with an evil-smelling fog that hovered some three or four feet above the ground. Ireland suggested that this, together with the bad quality of the water, gave the people severe agues and after several years of exposure they developed a yellowish complexion. Marshy ground harbours malaria-carrying mosquitoes that spread a debilitating illness known as 'the ague' or 'marsh fever', an English strain of malaria but less virulent than that found in the tropics. Those who contracted the ague rarely died of it but would have been incapacitated for a number of weeks. If during the period of convalescence, while still weak, the sufferer contracted another illness, death might follow. Despite this we can be quite sure there was a small settlement on the bank of the creek that would have stretched much further inland than it does today. There were similar settlements at Milton near its parish church and Murston; each was dependent on the creek for their livelihood. At this time the land mass would have been some 20ft lower than it is today so much of the northern Kent marshes would have been underwater and the local topography would have been very different from what we see today. Much of the county would have been covered by ancient forests, which is another reason why many people chose to live on its periphery, usually in coastal and riverine environments. Towns as we now recognise them are a Roman conception, so pre-Roman settlements would have been little more than enclosed and unenclosed homesteads and farms whose limits were demarcated by a ditch.

When studying the pre-Roman history of Sittingbourne it is important to remember that Watling Street did not exist; it was built some years after the Roman invasion of A.D. 43 to facilitate fast and easy access between the Channel ports, London and beyond. But that's not to say there were no track ways across Kent prior to the Roman invasion. There are many narrow country lanes, mostly on a north-south alignment, across the county, some of which were established long before the Roman invasion while others were later Saxon drove roads, built when they moved in on a well-established Iron-Age and Roman agricultural and industrial landscape. One such track way still to be seen is the Lower Road, running from at least the Roman fort, Reculver, near Herne Bay, to Rochester, crossing the River Medway at Cuxton en route to Southwark, a crossing point of the River Thames. The importance of this road is evidenced by the fact Murston, Teynham, Oare and Faversham are all sited on it; only Sittingbourne migrated northwards to take advantage of the opportunities Watling Street had to offer. At Teynham the remains of an archbishop's palace as

well as a Roman villa have been found but when studying Teynham it should be remembered that it once stood on the lower road; what we now call Teynham is actually Green Street, a reference to Watling Street, which runs through it having gone out of use and become grassed over.

Our ancestors relied considerably on water-borne travel and access to the sea was important for trading purposes. Even as late as the medieval period, a large proportion of inland trade went by river, far more than has ever been generally realised. Along the northern Kent coastline there are several coastal settlements that developed into small river-ports – Lower Halstow, Milton, Sittingbourne, Teynham, Conyer and Faversham. Of these, only Milton and Faversham developed into significant ports, Faversham more so than Milton. There is evidence of harbours and ships still awaiting excavation at Teynham, Luddenham, Conyer and Oare. The Swale and the creeks off it would all have been much wider in pre-Roman times and the lower road probably followed the shoreline as it still does along certain stretches. The creeks were fed by some sizeable rivers that flowed off the North Downs but they have long since dried up, leaving deep valleys scarring the landscape as at Stockbury, Borden Lane, Ufton Lane, Bell Road, either side of Newington and, away to the east, Syndale Bottom near Faversham. It has been suggested that the Highsted River which once flowed down the Highsted valley was navigable as far up as Highsted Farm.

We have scant archaeological evidence of early occupation of this area due to the widescale stripping back of the land's surface in the 19th century when brick earth was being dug out. It is said valuable-looking finds were unearthed from time to time but the workmen who found them

5   *Highsted valley, through which the river that flowed down Bell Road and Crown Quay Lane once went. It was here that amateur archaeologist Lesley Feakes found evidence of an early Iron-Age settlement.*

pocketed them to sell later. An ornate, valuable Roman lead coffin was excavated in one brick field, for example, but before local antiquary George Payne could rescue it the landowner, George Smeed, had it melted down and used the fine-quality lead to seal the gas pipes he was laying in town. There is evidence that the area was settled in during the Iron and Bronze Ages from an Iron-Age cemetery discovered in a chalk quarry at Highsted in 1955, and in 1928 a looped and socketed Bronze-Age axe was excavated in Ruins Barn Road. The Highsted quarry site contained 20 skeletons and six cremations, Belgic pottery and a La Tene brooch, the sole dating evidence. Unfortunately, pottery shards and drawings taken of the excavation were stolen so no report was ever published; the only records left are six photos taken by one of the excavators and local press reports.

Between 1871 and 1878 circular pits 10ft in diameter and between three and four feet deep were discovered at Grovehurst, Kemsley. Nearby, Celtic flint weapons were excavated; it is possible that these pits are the remains of Neolithic roundhouses. Prior to the construction of a new housing estate at Iwade in 2001, the remains of a previously unknown Iron-Age settlement were uncovered; over 3,000 artefacts were excavated. Subsequent research showed that the settlement, which included clearly defined farming enclosures and evidence of domestic dwellings, had been occupied for at least four thousand years.

Between 1998 and 2003 a programme of archaeological investigation at a new housing development at Kemsley was conducted by the Canterbury Archaeological Trust, who found evidence of late Mesolithic to early Bronze-Age activity, indicated by

6 *The quarry in the Highsted valley where in the 1950s an Iron-Age cemetery was discovered.*

residual lithic artefacts, but there were no archaeological features dating from this period. Features that were noted dated from the middle Bronze Age onwards. The earliest phase consisted of a single narrow ditch, thought to be part of an agricultural field system, a hypothesis supported by a scatter of pits and post-holes throughout the site, thought to be related to the field system. Settlement was suggested by two possible roundhouses and a fire pit or oven. There was also a square enclosure that truncated both the later field system and the narrow ditch. Activity appeared to have continued into the late Bronze Age.

Between 1874 and 1876 six lead coffins were discovered at Backs Hill, Milton Regis, one of which was highly ornamented, indicating that it belonged to someone of high status. At the time only 36 lead coffins had been found in the whole of Britain so the find of six at Milton Regis was more than on any other site. In

1889 there was another significant find to the north of the cemetery site – a gold finger ring set with red cornelian and a winged cupid drawing a two-horse chariot. It was a further indication of the wealth of those who once lived here. In 1879 a Roman walled cemetery was discovered by workmen digging out brick earth in a field said to be 'on the south side of Watling Street, one mile west of Sittingbourne near where the turnpike gate-keeper's house formerly stood'. It was thought that the cemetery may have been in use from the second to the fourth centuries A.D. In it the excavators found a small lead coffin containing a child's skeleton, two gold armillae, a ring of jet and a gold finger ring as well as a lead ossuarium and a cremation urn; the grave also contained several pieces of pottery. Later that same month, a second Roman interment was discovered there.

Several gold coins from the reign of Cunobelin, an Iron-Age chieftain, were dug up in College Road in 1950 and elsewhere in 1951, and one of Claudius Caesar was excavated at Tunstall in 1874. Cunobelin ruled over the Catuvellauni and Trinovantes tribes of southern England from *c.*A.D. 10 to 40. Britain was the last European region to adopt coinage and they first appeared here in *c.*150 B.C. Soon after, distinctive tribal examples were struck and to begin with they may have been used for gift exchange and votive offerings. It was only after Julius Caesar's incursions of 55 and 54 B.C. that diversity and denomination began to appear, factors that may reflect the emergence of a monetary system.

In 1877 a grave was discovered to the east of Bayford Orchard containing a Roman interment green glass vessel, a copper goblet, a bronze lamp, a copper jug, a glass jug, a copper bowl and a set of bathing implements. Two years later a second grave was discovered containing a thick blue glass vessel, a greenish-blue jug, a circular glass bottle, a bronze vase, an iron lamp stand, a pottery cup, a red clay pitcher, Samian ware and an urn-shaped Upchurch pottery-ware vase. Between November and December 1999, during the construction of the Eurolink Industrial Estate at Murston, Iron-Age pottery and Roman domestic debris dating from the mid- to late first century A.D. was discovered. Together with a number of pits it was clearly indicative of the presence of a small settlement that lay north of Watling Street, near the old lower road and adjacent to the creek, so it would have benefited from two major transport links.

It highlights the fact that this area was occupied long before the Roman invasion of A.D. 43. According to the antiquarian William Lambarde, Kent was the first inhabited part of Britain, probably because it is the closest point to the continent. It was populated since the earliest of times by the Celts, an ancient race of people, but Caesar's incursions in 55 and 54 B.C. are generally considered to be the time when Britain stepped upon the stage of history and came to prominence. After A.D. 43 and once Watling Street had been built, there is strong evidence of Roman influence here, with burials and villa-building along the road's entire length. Typical of this is the villa excavated at Boxted Farm, Newington in 1882. The walls measured almost 200ft in length and the building was 23ft wide. It had a tessellated pavement, or mosaic floor, and frescoes painted on the walls; it was clearly once the home of a wealthy landowner. Bapchild is another place where evidence of Roman occupation was discovered in 1929 and 1953. Further excavation of the site took place in 1972 when more domestic artefacts were found. From the evidence, archaeologists deduced that the site was in use from just before the Roman invasion of A.D. 43 until at least the third century. The landowner raised livestock, smelted and worked iron and lived on the site.

None of this indicates that there was a settlement of any description in Sittingbourne itself but that's not to say there wasn't one. Due to urban and industrial developments no traces of any ancient buildings have yet been found in the town. Sittingbourne's unique position on the London to Dover road, which later made it a convenient overnight stopping place for the pilgrims and mail coaches, would have similarly applied to the Roman legions that would quite possibly have had an overnight marching fort here, but evidence for it has never been found. Unlike other settlements, such as Rochester and Canterbury, neither Sittingbourne nor Milton ever became Roman towns despite there being evidence that some of the locals enjoyed a Romanised lifestyle. If the Romans had a fort here it should be considered that perhaps a *vicus* developed close by, where itinerant tradespeople would gather to serve the army's needs, selling them pots, pans and food and repairing their leather-ware and armour. This is only my own theory for which there is no firm evidence, other than it is known that such settlements did develop outside many institutions like forts, castles and monasteries etc. and this was how many towns began.

It's only after the Romans left Britain in A.D. 410 and the Anglo-Saxons arrived in the fifth to sixth centuries that tangible evidence starts to show that the area was inhabited. By A.D. 450 these Teutonic tribesmen from northern Europe had begun settling here. It was a piecemeal invasion with no overall plan for conquest and occupation. In the absence of any written records, something that gave rise to our referring to this as 'the Dark Ages', our knowledge of what was happening is based mainly on archaeological finds, the study of place-names and conjecture. It is well known, for example, that in A.D. 449 Kent was under constant attack by the Anglo-Saxons so King Vortigern enlisted the help of two Jutish leaders, Hengist and Horsa, promising them the Isle of Thanet in payment for services rendered. But how much of this is fact or fiction? Without written records it cannot be checked. It was not until 300 years later that the Venerable Bede, in his *Ecclesiastical History of England*, referred to the invaders of Kent as being Jutes, distinguishing them from the Angles who settled in East Anglia and the Saxons who settled in Essex, Sussex, Middlesex and Wessex. There were large-scale migrations of peoples on the continent during the fifth century and, faced by these savage invaders, most of

the indigenous population fled westward; others were killed or were taken into slavery. Fifth-century Kent was sparsely populated, possibly less than one fiftieth of what it is now.

Anglo-Saxon graves were discovered to the east of Milton Creek in 1824 and 1826; they were of the type used by prosperous yeoman farmers. But two of them contained a shield boss and a small dagger, signifying that they were warriors. Another contained a female skeleton with grave goods. The field in which they lay buried had never been ploughed so the skeletons were well preserved. In 1928 more cremation urns were found on this same site. Between 1869 and 1871 20 skeletons were exhumed from a Saxon cemetery discovered in a field on the corner of Hollybank Hill and Chalkwell Road, part of the Rondeau estate; six more were excavated in 1880. This field was never excavated for its brick earth and has long been built upon so it could be that there are more skeletons awaiting discovery beneath the houses which were later built there. Two more Anglo-Saxon inhumations with grave goods were discovered nearby in March 1882. When building work was being undertaken at the paper mill in 1872, a late Saxon scramasax, or knife inlaid with copper, bronze, silver and niello, measuring 12.75in by 1.375in with a 3in tang and inscribed 'Geberht owns me and Biorthelm made me', was found.

From this evidence it would seem conclusive that the Saxons settled here, but could it be that the centre of Saxon Sittingbourne was at Chalkwell rather than at the head of the creek, where it has long been thought the town originated? A chapel and hermitage called Schamel once stood on the corner of West Street and Ufton Lane, around which a small settlement referred to

7 *The* Volunteer *pub in West Street as seen in 1972. The Schamel chapel once stood here but no trace of it has ever been discovered. The pub has since been demolished and houses have been built on the site. [Fred Atkins]*

as Sittingbourne Parva developed. The earliest reference to this is contained in a document drawn up by Eleanor of Provence, the queen of Henry III, in *c.*1287. It would have stood on the banks of the stream or river that flowed down Ufton Lane into Cockleshell Walk, now the beginning of St Michael's Road, and the Chalkwell Road Saxon cemetery could well have been a part of it. In 1927, while workmen were digging deep pits for the underground petrol tanks of the filling station on the corner of Dover Street, they discovered a large number of human bones, including two complete skeletons. One of them showed signs of having suffered a violent death. It was conjectured

at the time that they were the remains of passing pilgrims who had been attacked. Could this site have once been a part of a graveyard attached to the Schamel chapel?

But there are two important pieces of evidence to support the claim that Sittingbourne developed from a small settlement located on the bank of the creek in Crown Quay Lane. This was where Bayford castle, of which there are now no traces left, was built and Bayford Court manor house, said once to have been the home of Earl Godwin, the Earl of Kent and father of King Harold in the 11th century, but which one of the two was the ancestral home, no one is quite sure. The castle would have been an awesome

8   *Crown Quay where the early hamlet of Sittingbourne began. Tied up is the barge* Sir Wilfred Lawson, *registered in Rochester.*

9   *The head of Milton Creek, 1999, looking much narrower than it was in years gone by. [Mick Clancy]*

and dominating structure, towering over the tiny hamlet, and it probably quickly became the central focus of the area, as an estate and manorial centre where the local court was held. English Heritage has suggested a possible date for the castle as being pre-1368 and the Ordnance Survey map of 1869/71 offers a date of A.D. 892, when the Viking leader Haesten arrived in Milton, which ties in with the long-held myth that King Alfred built Bayford Castle, from where he could monitor the Vikings' movements. It has no supporting evidence.

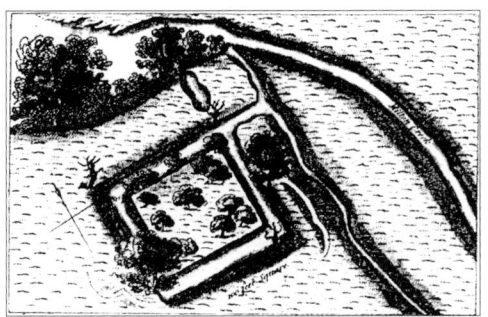

10   *Plan of Castle Rough, Kemsley as seen and sketched by Edward Hasted c.1798 when he visited the site. Today the site looks much the same as it did then but, despite extensive archaeological research, including excavation, no trace of Viking occupation has ever been found.* [Courtesy of Local History Publications]

According to the Anglo-Saxon chronicles, in A.D. 892 Haesten set sail from Boulogne with an estimated 330 ships laden with men and horses to plunder Kent. The force divided in mid-Channel with 250 ships heading for Appledore while the remaining 80 set off for Milton where it is said they built a fort, Castle Rough. Despite the site being a Scheduled Ancient Monument, archaeological excavations have so far been unable to find any Viking artefacts or traces of the fort's earthworks. Personally speaking, I do not see the Castle Rough site as being the archetypal shape for a Viking stronghold; it is more akin to a medieval moated manor site. I believe the site of Castle Rough lies beneath the foundations of the nearby paper mill. Edward Hasted was convinced that the site we can see today was the Viking stronghold when he visited it sometime between 1788 and 1799 while compiling his *History and Topographical Survey of Kent.* He described it as being '... of a square form, surrounded by a high bank thrown up, and a broad ditch. There was a raised causeway leading from it to the foreshore.' This does sound very much like the site we have today and his sketch of it bears a remarkable resemblance but the archetypal shape of all Viking forts is 'D'-shaped, the

upright part of the letter being the river or waterway upon which the fort would have been built. Christopher Saxon's 1590 map of Goodneston manor shows the site of the castle and refers to it as 'castle ruffe' but it has long been accepted that Castle Rough is at Kemsley.

Bayford Castle and Goodneston (also known as Goodmanston and Godewynston) were separate manors but appear to have been held by the same lord from c.1368. The first person to hold both manors was Robert de Nottingham who resided at Bayford and dated several of his deeds '*apud castellum suum de Bayford, apud Goodneston*'. From this it may be conjectured that the capital residence was at Bayford manor while the Goodneston manor house became derelict and the manor itself lost much of its separate identity. The association of Bayford Castle, presumably the Goodneston manor house site where Earl Godwin lived, with the date A.D. 892 would appear to stem from Camden and has no basis in fact. Could it be, therefore, that Bayford Castle was not the overly impressive structure that we have come to think of castles as being but simply a moated enclosure that grew

11   *Bayford Court manor house, 1995. [Barry Kinnersley]*

12   *Part of the moat that surrounds Bayford Court, 2002. [Mick Clancy]*

13 *St Michael's Church, 1907, the town's original, and for many centuries only, church.*

in size and importance after the Normans arrived? Bayford Court might have been identical to Bayford Castle but it cannot be concluded they were the same structures. It is thought that, by the end of the 15th century, the castle had ceased to be a viable defensive measure and had by then been reduced to being a farm house – or was this Bayford Court that was being referred to? It's an enigma that continues to puzzle local historians. The manor house we can see today dates back to *c.*1700 but internally there are the remains of an earlier half-timbered building and it is surrounded on three sides by a moat. For such an ancient structure surprisingly little is known about Bayford Castle. One final theory is that Bayford Castle might well have been the site of the original Roman

marching camp built when the legions were passing through. It lay close to the original main road. After they left, the local chieftain could have taken it over and, in time, developed it into a high-status site; this was not an uncommon practice. I have no firm evidence to support this, of course.

After Harold's defeat at Hastings William confiscated many English estates and distributed them among his loyal followers. He made his brother, Bishop Odo of Bayeux, the Earl of Kent, and granted him much of the land in this area, including the castle and manor of Tonge, which he in turn passed on to Hugh de Port who is mentioned in Domesday Book. On the corner of Crown Quay Lane and Watling Street stands the town's parish church, St Michael's, mostly of Norman construction, which probably replaced an earlier wooden Saxon church, so it would seem likely that this was the true original epicentre of our town.

Another theory that has been offered for consideration is perhaps that the town evolved from a collection of several small pre-Norman settlements scattered throughout what is now Sittingbourne. Throughout the town there are unrelated areas wherein there is evidence of early occupation. At Chalkwell, for instance, there is a house named Westfields whose origin is most definitely early medieval and across the road once stood a long-established tannery. Could this have once been an independent settlement? It was ideally situated on the crossroads of east-west traffic travelling along Watling Street and the north-south flow travelling from the outlying countryside to Milton market and port. At the other end of town is East Street which has several medieval buildings like the *Plough*, *Ship* and *Wheatsheaf* public houses and the shop on the corner of Canterbury Road and St Michael's Road. Buildings like these would not have necessarily stood in isolation but would have been part of a self-contained settlement.

It is conjectured that William, Duke of Normandy passed through Sittingbourne at the head of his army marching towards London after defeating King Harold in 1066. The victorious Normans marched firstly to Dover, then to Canterbury; London was their next goal but it is unclear which way they went. Some say they headed off down what is now the A28 towards the A20 road but the A2 would have been a more direct route and there are some tantalising clues to support this. The best historical account of the Norman invasion and its immediate aftermath

was written by William of Poitiers in his book *Gesta Guillelmi* soon after the event. In it, after describing the capitulation of Canterbury he said, 'Coming next day to the Broken Tower, the Duke pitched his camp. In that place he was afflicted by a severe illness, which caused great anxiety to his closest followers.' (*Gesta Guillelmi ii, 28;* translation from Davis and Chibnall, 1998.) The narrative is not clear on what and where the Broken Tower was and no other accounts of the invasion mention it so the site has never been positively identified. The text implies that the Broken Tower was an isolated landmark, away from any obvious settlement and in the context of the narrative it would appear that it lay somewhere beyond Canterbury. The section of Watling Street between Canterbury and Rochester does not pass through any major towns. Small settlements at Faversham, Teynham and Sittingbourne existed at that time but none is mentioned by William of Poitiers. The Broken Tower was, therefore, just a suitable place for an overnight roadside camp. It could once have been a part of a ruined Saxon church or the remains of a much older Roman structure, a more likely scenario as William of Poitiers, being a cleric, would have paid more attention had the structure been a church. There are several likely locations but in 1879 a walled Roman cemetery was discovered by local antiquary George Payne, which offered the best evidence yet of the Broken Tower's exact location. Mr Payne described the site as being '… one mile west of Sittingbourne where until very recently stood the turnpike house; the field behind this was excavated for brickearth'. It included the remains of a large tower that, from its foundations, measured 5ft 6in thick and 11ft 6in in diameter; given these dimensions, the foundations

14 *The Half-Mile Path, the remaining section of the conjectured droveway from the uplands of Kingsdown, through the Highsted valley and on to the market and port at Milton. [Mick Clancy]*

could have supported a structure some 30 or more feet high. Added to this can be the location; it was a good day's march (16 miles) from Canterbury. It was some 300 yards north of the stream that flowed down what is now Borden Lane and, as Milton was a royal demesne, food would have been plentiful for William's huge army. The excavators had little idea of the original purpose of the tower and today this site is covered by Adelaide Drive. As meagre as this 'evidence' may be, it does seem to be a likely candidate for the site of the mysterious Broken Tower.

Of Sittingbourne Parva, it came to nothing and probably disappeared once the Shamel hermitage and chapel were demolished. Today there are no traces of any buildings of any significant age in this area, unlike the High Street, which has many.

This, therefore, is what I believe to be the beginning of Sittingbourne, an ancient creek-side settlement inhabited by fishermen and traders who had come together through the various prehistoric ages, into the Roman era and emerging in Anglo-Saxon times ready for expansion. The original settlement was never a town or village; more like a tiny waterside hamlet. Once Watling Street was constructed the inhabitants realised its potential and relocated to take advantage of passing trade. Slowly the original creek-side settlement fell into disuse as the new location on Watling Street expanded. It is not uncommon for a settlement to move its point of focus. Changing economic and social factors often dictated this throughout history. Local instances include Milton, which moved from an unhealthy creek-side location beside the church to the hilltop site it occupies today, and Teynham, which like Sittingbourne moved southwards to take advantage of passing trade along Watling Street.

Chapter 2

Medieval and Post-Medieval Development

It was two seemingly insignificant and unrelated events that shaped the beginning of Sittingbourne's history and development – the Roman legacy of Watling Street and a chance comment made by King Henry II when he uttered those immortal words, 'Will no one rid me of this turbulent priest?', a reference to his close friend Archbishop Thomas Becket following a heated argument with him. It was the sort of comment many of us make in a moment of frustration or anger but on this occasion it was overheard by a group of Henry's loyal knights who sped off to Canterbury to assassinate him, thinking they were doing the king's bidding. And so, from 1170 onwards, visits to Becket's tomb in Canterbury Cathedral became one of the most popular pilgrimages in Britain and Western Europe as stories spread of miracles happening at his tomb. Many hundreds of pious pilgrims journeyed along Watling Street from Southwark to Canterbury and back, and it has been suggested that by 1420 over 100,000 had made the pilgrimage. But despite its Roman-designed directness the journey along Watling Street was long, arduous and dangerous, no matter whether you travelled on foot, on horseback or by coach.

Sittingbourne's close proximity to Canterbury and Rochester, together with being almost equidistant between London and the Channel ports, made it a convenient overnight stopping point on the long journey. At first the town did not have any inns or hostelries in which to accommodate travellers; they evolved later as a direct result of this passing trade,

which inspired Canon Scott Robertson, rector of Elmley, to describe Sittingbourne as 'a street of inns' in his 1879 book on Sittingbourne's history. As long-distance travel became more popular, monasteries, priories, abbeys and hospitals were established. To begin with most were quite small and, as well as undertaking their religious duties, the monks took care of the infirm and sick; they could also offer overnight accommodation to passing travellers. Sittingbourne had two religious hospitals, the Schamel hermitage and chapel dedicated to St Thomas Becket in West Street and the Hospital of St Leonard, attached to the chapel of the Holy Cross of Swainestrey at Snipeshill, where Rectory Road playing field now stands. The two establishments were complete opposites in character and little is now known about them except for a number of early dated deeds held by New College, Oxford, relating to the endowment of the chapel of the Holy Cross. Such was the scarcity of information that they were even overlooked by Edward Hasted and other Kentish historians, but in *Dugdale* (vol.VI, p.765; 1846) there's a reference to 'a grant being made to the master of the hospital of the Holy Cross to have a fair at the Chapel of Swinestre on the eve and day of Holy Cross', i.e. on 2 and 3 May. In *Archaeologia Cantiana* (vol.XXIX, p.255) Mr Hussey locates the chapel as being in the grounds of Murston rectory and cites a local will dated 1525 showing that the chapel was in use at that time. There are two surviving examples of these medieval hospitals not too far away; one is in Ospringe, known as the Maison Dieu, while the other is in Canterbury, known as The Canterbury Pilgrims' Hospital of St Thomas in St Peter's Street. They were nothing like the hospitals we have today; they simply offered overnight accommodation, a frugal meal and the opportunity to pray for a safe journey.

Schamel hermitage is said to have taken its name from a priest named Samuel who said daily mass and attended to the needs of passing travellers who, in return for his blessing, would make a small donation. It is not known exactly when it was set up but it certainly existed in 1255 when Henry III issued a writ demanding to know how much it and the four houses held by Brother Silvester, an Austin friar and hermit of St Augustine's, were worth. After Samuel died the hermitage and chapel fell into ruins but it was later rebuilt by an unknown Augustinian monk. He was succeeded by Walter de Hermestone who was appointed by Eleanor of Provence, the queen of Henry III, Lord of the Manor and Hundred of Middletun and patron of the chapel in 1271. Upon his arrival he found the townspeople, led by the priest of St Michael's Church, Simon de Shordich, had wrecked the chapel and stolen the bell and the altar to install in their own church. The townspeople saw the Schamel hermitage as a threat to their own livelihoods. If travellers gave their money there, they would have less to spend in the town. Soon after this incident Simon de Shordich died, said to be from the effects of the curses showered on him by Walter de Hermestone. Sixteen years later the queen, as patron of the tiny chapel, held an inquiry and it is from this record that we first hear of the small hamlet around the chapel referred to as Sittingbourne Parva. The chapel was rebuilt and little is known about it until June 1358 when the queen

of Edward III, Philippa of Hainault, gave 20 shillings in alms. At that time a friar by the name of Richard de Lexedon was in charge of the chapel. Two years later it is recorded that King John of France passed by on his way home and gave 20 nobles, or £120. The hermitage and chapel were demolished in c.1542.

St Leonard's hospital and the chapel of the Holy Cross of Swainestrey, on the other hand, was a larger establishment and thought more highly of than Schamel. Wealthy locals often left large sums of money in their wills for its maintenance and upkeep. It is thought that the original chapel was founded by the Lord of the Manor of Murston, Bartholomew de Morston, in an act of piety, a typical act by noblemen at this time who saw their generosity as a guarantee of going to heaven when they died. Throughout its life the advowson of the chapel was always treated as appendant to the manor. After it was demolished, probably during the Reformation, a rectory for Murston Church was built on the site but that too was demolished in the late 1940s to make way for a new housing estate.

It was not long before the townspeople began to realise there was a profitable living to be made from passing travellers and, as the accommodation at Schamel and Swainestrey was limited, they offered rooms in their homes for the night; no doubt they also took the opportunity to set up stalls to sell essential commodities. This was probably when the town moved to its present location. By 1340 Sittingbourne had become a well-established and accepted principal overnight halt on the journey to and from London. It is one of the few places mentioned by name in Chaucer's *Canterbury Tales* in the chapter 'Words between the Summoner and the Friar' and, in recognition of this, when the

15 *Maison Dieu, Ospringe near Faversham c.1890. There would have been many religious hospitals like this for travellers to use all over the country. Sittingbourne had two, Swainestry and Schamel; both have long been demolished but it's fair to say they probably looked something like this. See how Ospringe also has a stream cutting across the main road. [Courtesy of the Faversham Society]*

16 *Another pilgrims' hospital that still exists is in St Peter's Street, Canterbury. [Barry Kinnersley]*

Wetherspoon's pub opened at the end of the 1990s it was named the *Summoner*.

The focal point of the town for the pilgrims would have been St Michael's Church where, on its south-eastern corner, was a niche set in the buttress that contained a statue of the Virgin Mary, known as Our Lady of the Buttress. It was held in high esteem by the locals, many of whom asked to be buried close by when they died. In the will of Robert Wyborn, dated January 1473, for example, he requested, 'I be buried neare St Marie of the Boterasse' and similarly, in 1466, John Lotter left 6d. in his will to 'the little chapel of Blessed Mary at Botras'. Until 1765, there was a large wooden porch around the buttress where those hearing mass could shelter from the weather.

One of our earliest inns that still serves the town as a public house is the *Red Lion* and, according to Canon Scott Robertson in an address he gave to the Sittingbourne Literary and Scientific Association on 4 March 1878, '… it had been an inn of some note for more than 500 years'. It is our last remaining inn that is complete with its original stable yard. We know, for example, that King Henry V was entertained at the *Red Lion* in November 1415 on his return from the Battle of Agincourt by Sir John Northwode of Milton at a cost of 9s. 9d., but at that time wine was only 1d. per pint. Seven years later on 3 October 1422 his funeral cortège passed through the town. Henry died at Vincennes, France and his body was taken to Westminster Abbey, London. The cortège, led by King James I of Scotland and Henry's widow, Queen Catherine of Valois, halted while the coffin lay in state in several towns en route but at Sittingbourne a funeral service was held at St Michael's Church, conducted by the Bishop of Norwich, John de Wakering. The accounts of King Henry VIII show

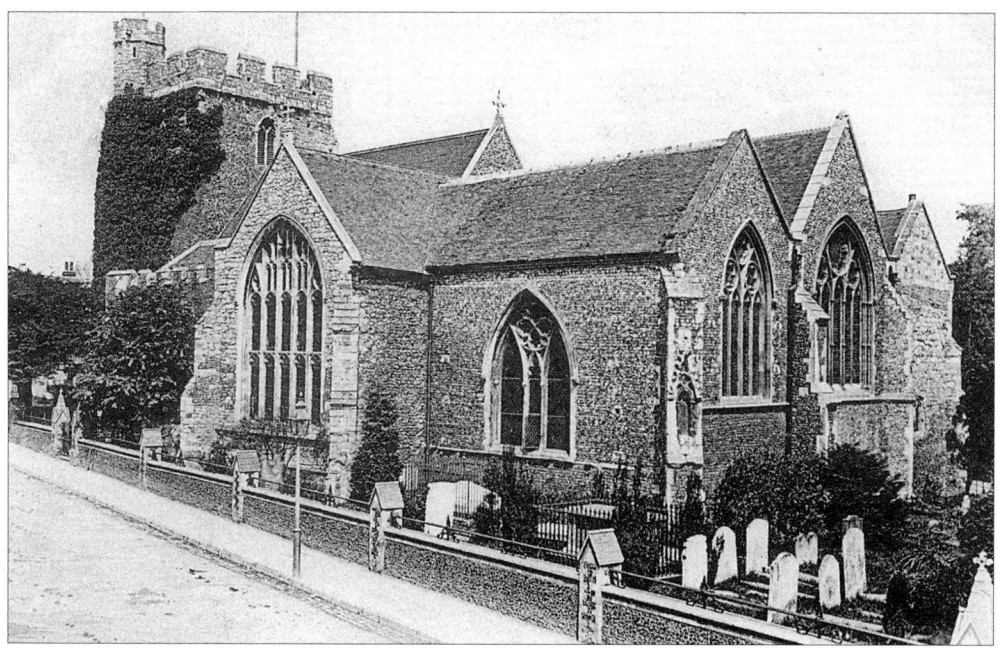

17 *St Michael's Church, showing the niche on its south-eastern corner wherein once stood a statue of St Mary, a site much revered by the medieval pilgrims as they passed through the town as well as the local population.*

that in November 1532 he paid the landlord of the *Red Lion* the sum of 4s. 8d. for overnight accommodation for his servants and followers. One of the most spectacular cavalcades to pass through the town was that of King Henry VIII and the Hapsburg Emperor Charles V in May 1532. Local noblemen John Cheney of Ufton Court, Sir William Cromer of Tunstall and Sir John Northwode of Milton were instructed to find lodgings for the 2,000-strong contingent.

A later owner of the *Red Lion* was Sir William Garrett who, in 1555, had been Lord Mayor of London. With such a lucrative and regal clientèle, it was said that the landlords of the *Red Lion* often cocked their noses at princes and archbishops and even turned away dukes and earls. It was indeed a prestigious place to stay and no doubt whenever anyone of any importance came here the innkeepers would have been overjoyed as it meant a guaranteed income for them in return for board and lodging. Someone who might not have been so favourably received by the town was Marie de Medicis, Queen of France and mother-in-law of Charles I. She came here in 1644 and is thought to have stayed at the *Red Lion* for three nights. At that time the French were not among our best friends.

Another former inn, of which today only the High Street frontage remains, is the *Bull* but, despite this, it still serves the town as a public house. Little research has been conducted into its past but it is thought to have been licensed originally by the monks of Chilham Castle in the 12th century. Hence its name does not have a bovine connection but is linked rather to the papal bull. It has been suggested that it was functioning as an inn as early as 1562 when it was purchased by Richard Rolens from John Fowle; the remains of

18 *The* Red Lion *inn stable yard sketched in the 1960s. [David Colthup]*

the present building date back to *c.*1750. Until the construction of Roman Square in the 1970s, the *Bull* and its many outbuildings stretched back from the High Street and connected with the town's cattle market, formerly Bull Meadows, where the Swallows Leisure Centre car park now stands.

The third of our principal coaching inns was the *George*, of which only its tap house or public bar remains, now called the *Entertainer*. Parts of this inn date back to *c.*1685. Architecturally it has wooden eaves, cornice and wide sash boxes set flush into the brickwork, which is typical for the period of construction. Following the Great Fire of London in 1666, many generally accepted architectural features like those incorporated into the *George* were seen as potential fire hazards so, in 1707 and 1709, legislative measures were taken for sashes to be set back behind four inches of brickwork and cornices to be replaced by a brick parapet so that the

wall would extend above roof level. The actual hotel originally occupied what are now the Blundell's furnishers and D & A Sports shops. At first the hotel was named the *George and Dragon* but it ceased to be a hotel in the early 18th century when the Lushington family purchased it and converted it into a grand town house. Here they often entertained King Georges I and II as they travelled between London and Germany. The adjoining tap house, originally known as the *Bell*, is thought to have been renamed the *George* in honour of the royal connection. It still has its original carriage arch running through into Banks Yard where a mysterious section of flint wall can be seen on its western side. Could this be the remains of an earlier building? The stable yard of the *George* is reckoned once to have been large enough to accommodate 40 horses.

There is a noticeable absence of any really ancient buildings in Sittingbourne and this might be explained by a period known

19 *High Street showing the location of inns such as the* Bull, *the* Rose *and the* Red Lion.

20 *The* George *inn, the remaining taphouse of the once much larger* George Hotel. *This pub has recently been renamed* The Entertainer. *[David Colthup]*

21 *Once a pub called* Sweepstakes *and later the* Bell, *this building later became Featherstone's departmental store but retained the name and sign of Bell House. After its demolition it became a car park and today the site is occupied by McCarthy Stone's retirement homes. [Courtesy of Chris Deamer]*

22 *Bell Road, looking towards the High Street, 1975. [Fred Atkins]*

to historians as the Great Rebuilding. It has never been fully documented; the evidence for it is almost entirely in the field and contained in probate inventories of this time. Between about 1570 and 1630 important social changes took place, which included the modernisation and enlarging of houses at nearly every social level. This could possibly be the time when much of modern-day Sittingbourne was originally built.

Previously written books about the history of Sittingbourne tell of an almost seamless transition from the pilgrim trade to coach travel to the coming of the railway and our industrial heritage. They suggest that the town met and overcame each change almost effortlessly but a devastating national event occurred in the mid-17th century. Nothing had been written about its local impact and consequences until 2005.

In 1665–6 a plague epidemic swept across Britain, annihilating much of the population. It was not the first such epidemic to affect Britain but it is the one of which we know the most. Hardly a single town or village escaped its effects but somehow it did not affect Sittingbourne to any degree. This 340-year-old mystery was discovered by local historian Alan Abbey who, in 2005–6, wrote about his findings for his university thesis. The burial records of St Michael's Church for 1665–6 show that very few local people died of the plague; the total number of burials was closer to the town's normal yearly average.

Significantly more people are recorded as dying of the plague in 1610 and 1615-16. The records identify Jude Sturgeon, who died on 14 September 1665, as being the most likely person to have brought the disease to Sittingbourne. A note in the records reveals that he '… brought the sickness', which he then passed on to his wife, who died on 4 October, and possibly his daughter Sarah, whose death on the same day carries no further details. On 5 November 1665 Henry Butler is recorded as dying 'of the sickness', and the same was said of two females named Martha Butler (mother and daughter?) who died on 13 and 14 November, and Mary Beechinge, Mr Sturgeon's servant, who died on 7 December, presumably also of the plague.

Why did Sittingbourne escape so lightly? After all, being on the main London to Dover road and being at the head of a waterway giving good access to the River Thames and London, it would seem logical to assume that this highly infectious disease would have hit this area hard. The constant flow of travellers passing through would have added to the risk but, according to the records, only a handful of people are registered as dying of the plague whereas elsewhere hundreds were dying daily. Mr Abbey concluded that there was a subtle change taking place in the traditional role Sittingbourne had played during the earlier years of the medieval period. As commercial traffic began increasingly to use the ports of Rochester, Milton and Faversham, travel by road went into decline. Increasingly water-borne traffic to Milton bypassed Sittingbourne and, being less than a mile away, few people would have stopped at Sittingbourne, whose quays were inadequate for the larger vessels of the period. It was more a base for local fishermen than for handling imports and exports. The lack of suitable port facilities was an economic setback for Sittingbourne but the town benefited from new commercial opportunities even though they took a while to be realised. The major cause of the plague spreading was through trade, i.e. flea-infected textiles, wool, hides and straw, and being carried by rodents, especially the black rat, but, as Sittingbourne had little contact with major cities and ports, it limited the town's contact with potential sources.

Stepping back a few years to 1652, Sittingbourne was at an all-time economic low, unable even to support its own poor. This situation had been going on for a number of years and is highlighted in the town's charter of 1599. In 1653 the Justices of the quarter sessions court ordered the parish of Elmley to help out by paying Sittingbourne £12 a year, an arrangement that continued until 1658. At that time Elmley was a successful and thriving village on the bank of the Swale. Today nothing remains except for a collection of humps and bumps in the landscape where its houses and public buildings once would have been. Few visitors ventured into poverty-stricken Sittingbourne, so it is conjectured that this is another reason why the plague little affected the town.

By 1664 the hearth tax returns show that Sittingbourne's economic situation was improving and the town had few poor people and a surprising proportion of more substantial buildings, many of which were inns with which the town had long been associated. A list of towns with the number of beds and stable places available in each of them was published in 1686, leaving little doubt that Sittingbourne had successfully returned to its traditional role of hospitality. At this time the suggested population of Sittingbourne was 500, compared with Milton, which had about

850; Sittingbourne had 101 inn beds whereas Milton had just thirty-three. This trend extended into the 18th century when in 1708 a new hotel, the *Rose*, was built in Sittingbourne, described by Edward Hasted as '… the most superb of any throughout the kingdom'.

This suggests that Sittingbourne should have been exposed to a far greater risk of the plague. If a town is regularly visited by a large number of strangers the risk of them bringing the plague to the town should surely increase. It is hard to envisage a scenario in which Sittingbourne could have avoided a plague crisis, especially as other local towns did not. It can only be concluded that the plague radiated out from London and, as Sittingbourne was not a major port, it had little direct contact with the capital. As the number of travellers using Watling Street fell, the risk of the plague being brought into the town was greatly reduced and, as the town was not reliant upon trade and commercial connections, it was able to recover far faster than those that were.

Surviving records from the medieval period show that there was considerable local interest and involvement in national events at this time, the local population being kept abreast of developments by passing travellers. In 1381, for example, Wat Tyler rebelled against a tax introduced by Richard II to raise money for his war against France. His peasant army marched on London to demand changes in the agricultural system, which at that time included serfdom. The *Presentment of Malefactors* records those who rose up against the king including '… William Brown of Bixle [near Bredgar] and John Webbe of Maidstone who slew John Godwot of Borden and also John Smyth of Tunstall, who with others slew John Tebbe at Canterbury'. It goes on to tell how:

> … on 10 June 1381 John Hales of Malling, Walter Teghelere of Essex and other malefactors made assault on William Septvantz, Sheriff of Kent, dragged him to prison and forced him to go to his manor at Milton and made him swear that he would deliver up all rolls and writs in his custody. This he did under fear of death and John Hales burnt them.

Two more significant events that each played a major part in the lives of Kentish people took place in the 15th century, each of which involved people from Sittingbourne. The first was John Cade's Rebellion in 1450, at a time of an increasingly unstable royal government leading to growing anarchy. The people of Kent suffered under the harsh treatment of local tyrants like Lord Saye & Sele, and his son-in-law Sir William Crowmer of Tunstall, Sheriff of Kent. Angered beyond all reason, Cade rebelled against King Henry VI and according to the patent rolls:

> … a substantial number of the local townsfolk, as well as those from the agricultural community, were involved. Three Gentlemen, John Goolde, Richard Grovehurst and John Buntyn of Milton were followers of Cade, as were the Tonges, yeoman farmers, and six husbandmen. Eleven members of the local fishing community took part, including Wills Maas and Will and John Colke.

Also mentioned are a butcher, a smith, a fuller, a cordwainer, a tanner, a barbour, a bereman and a roper. The rebels marched on London and, after seizing Saye & Sele and Crowmer, beheaded them both. Mission accomplished, they returned home and were later pardoned for their crime but not before '… being paraded before the King, bare-chested and with a noose around their necks'. This incident captured the public's imagination and Shakespeare makes mention of Saye & Sele, Crowmer, Cade and some of their followers in *Henry VI, Part II*.

The 15th century was a time when England was embroiled in the Wars of the Roses. In 1471 Sir Thomas Fauconberge, the bastard son of William Neville, Earl of Kent and a keen supporter of the House of Lancaster, landed in Kent with a mercenary army in an attempt to rescue the former King Henry VI from the Tower of London. Fauconberg is said to have sent a letter, dated 8 May 1471, from Sittingbourne to the Commonalty of the City of London, requesting them not to prevent him from entering the city. His request was denied so Fauconberg's army attacked London and set fire to London Bridge. As King Edward IV advanced on Fauconberg's mercenaries, they retreated back into Kent, heading towards Sandwich. Edward IV gave chase as far as Canterbury and later, following the death of Henry VI, Fauconberg surrendered. There is no mention of any Sittingbourne people being among Fauconberg's army but it is fair to assume that he could have picked up the odd local here and there as he passed through the area.

In the 1550s, during the reign of Queen Mary, Sir Thomas Wyatt led an unsuccessful attempt to put Elizabeth on the throne, following Mary's announcement of her intention to marry Philip of Spain. Wyatt was supported by Sir William Crowmer of Tunstall who escaped the scaffold but was instead sent to the Tower and had his lands confiscated. He was released after a couple of months and in a little over a year his lands were restored to him.

The Civil War little affected this part of England; the main battles were to the north and the west of London. Sittingbourne was predominantly sympathetic towards Parliament but there were a number of local gentry suspected of being pro-Royalist, including Edward Hales of Tunstall, John Throwling of Milton and Robert Barham and Paul Graunt, both of Sittingbourne, but Lord Thomas Fairfax, Captain-General of the Parliamentary forces, was convinced that Edward Hales's grandfather, Sir Edward Hales, was not involved in the Royalist cause so he ordered all confiscated property to be restored to him. Shortly before the execution of Charles I in January 1649 there was a Royalist uprising in Kent when Edward Hales of Tunstall and Sir James Hales of Canterbury, a distant relation, presented a petition to Parliament. Edward had been appointed General of the Royalist army, which consisted of about 5,000–6,000 foot soldiers and 1,000 horsemen. They seized magazines and arms as well as the castles at Queenborough and Dover before marching to Blackheath, just outside London, where they presented the petition. The Earl of Norfolk then replaced Edward Hales, who took no further part in the war, as General.

Chapter 3

Early Urban Growth

Sittingbourne continued to be over-shadowed by Milton for many centuries. According to a survey undertaken in 1566, there were 93 houses in Sittingbourne and 136 in Milton. Both were recognised as separate towns, each with their own different economy. One of the earliest property transactions we have is contained in the will of John Pykyll, dated 1530, who left to John Row, his '… house and garden in the town of Syttyngbourne'. In his book *A New and Complete History of the County of Kent,* W.H. Ireland reminds us '… although Milton is paramount over the parish of Sittingbourne, it has four subordinate manors – Goodneston, Bayford, Chilton and Fulston'.

Throughout the 15th century Watling Street was maintained in good order and was described by Ogilby in his book *Britannia* in 1675 as '… a very good and well beaten way, chiefly chalky and gravelly, and none better provided for conveniency of entertainment, being the most frequented road in England'. Bequests for its upkeep were often included in the wills of wealthy local people. In the 16th century it took five days to travel the 71 miles from London to Dover with overnight stops at Dartford, Rochester, Sittingbourne and Canterbury. By the 18th century it was still Sittingbourne's geographical position that dominated the town's economy as faster stage coaches were introduced, cutting the journey time down to one-and-a-half days with only one overnight stop, and that was at Sittingbourne. In 1726 King George II travelled from Hythe directly to Sittingbourne without making the usual overnight stop at Canterbury. This was the great age of stage-coach travel and Sittingbourne's place in Kent's social and commercial life was at its peak. Inns made changes to cope with the growth in stage-coach travel and whereas in a will dated 1707 it was said '… the *Red Lyon* had stables', by 1780 it was said to have 'coach houses'.

The growth of Sittingbourne as a coaching centre continued throughout the 17th and 18th centuries. Many of the innkeepers were by now local gentry or businessmen who could supply from their farms the produce the inns needed. This was a departure from the earlier practice whereby the inns were generally run by tenants. Evidence from the 18th-century records of Sittingbourne's licensed victuallers shows that there was a high percentage of medium and long-term licence holders, indicating that the economy of the town supported a fairly large and stable innkeeping fraternity. However, the list of licensed innkeepers does not give a full picture of the trade within the town's economy; many doubtlessly operated without licences.

As the town started to grow it was administered by the Vestry, a body consisting of representatives who organised parish business, including the day-to-day management of the church through two churchwardens, care of the poor through two overseers and maintenance of local roads and highways. The Vestry had no control over the town's planning and layout, relying instead on the good sense of those who built new houses. By 1573 the people of Sittingbourne considered their town important enough for official recognition and took the opportunity to request Queen Elizabeth I for incorporation while she was passing through the town. It was granted and gave the town a limited degree of self-government, the right to raise revenue through a rating system, the right to hold a weekly market and two annual fairs and representation in Parliament but, following opposition from the people of Milton who thought a market in Sittingbourne would be detrimental to their own ancient rights, it was revoked. There is, however, a suggestion of where that early market might have been held. It can be seen that the High Street widens somewhat just beyond the *George* [or *Entertainer*] inn. This is a common enough feature in most medieval market towns. A second application for a charter was made in 1599 and it was granted in a more modified form with the emphasis on the town's role as an overnight resting place for travellers. The charter was granted partly because some of the more influential locals wanted to protect their trade of supplying the needs of travellers. On the authority of their first charter the townspeople were instructed to '... refuse that the victuallers of the town should enter into bond for not killing, eating and uttering of flesh during Lent'. This was opposed and the success of the action in defending the town's economy is clear in that Robert Netter, a butcher, was one of those 'sent for by warrant to answer objections to their actions', and, far from being penalised, was named as a jurat of the town in its second charter.

Wills drawn up in the late 15th and early 16th centuries describe both Sittingbourne and Milton as being market and manufacturing centres. Apart from Sandwich, Canterbury and Faversham, Sittingbourne and Milton were the only market towns in this rich agricultural area of northern Kent but, following Milton's protestations, Sittingbourne's market was closed down by a State Decree of Court. Being a one-street town, ideal for the inns that dominated its economy, there was no advantage in Sittingbourne trying to hold a market, especially as Milton's was so close by. It would have made life very difficult for the coach drivers if they had to negotiate market stalls while trying to turn into the stable yards. Much of Sittingbourne's requirements for produce were to supply its inns, rather than the small-scale needs of private households. Such requirements could be more easily satisfied directly by local farmers who in many cases also owned the inns. Sittingbourne's burial registers for 1650–9 show that around forty per cent of the town's workforce was engaged in occupations of one sort or another that satisfied the needs of passing travellers. The importance of innkeeping to the town's economy continued until the 19th century.

An Extract from The Sittingbourne Charter of 1599.
Elizabeth, by the Grace of God, Queen of England, France and Ireland, defender of the faith. To all those present, letters shall come, greetings.

As the inhabitants of the town and parish of Sittingbourne in the county of Kent, being in great ruins and decay, have most humbly beseeched us for help and assistance and relief from the great burdens and expenses which they bear from time to time ... by receiving and lodging in the houses of the inhabitants ... many right honourable and worthy men, our ambassadors and couriers and their mounted attendants ... by providing horses and other necessary things ... for which it is most suited ...

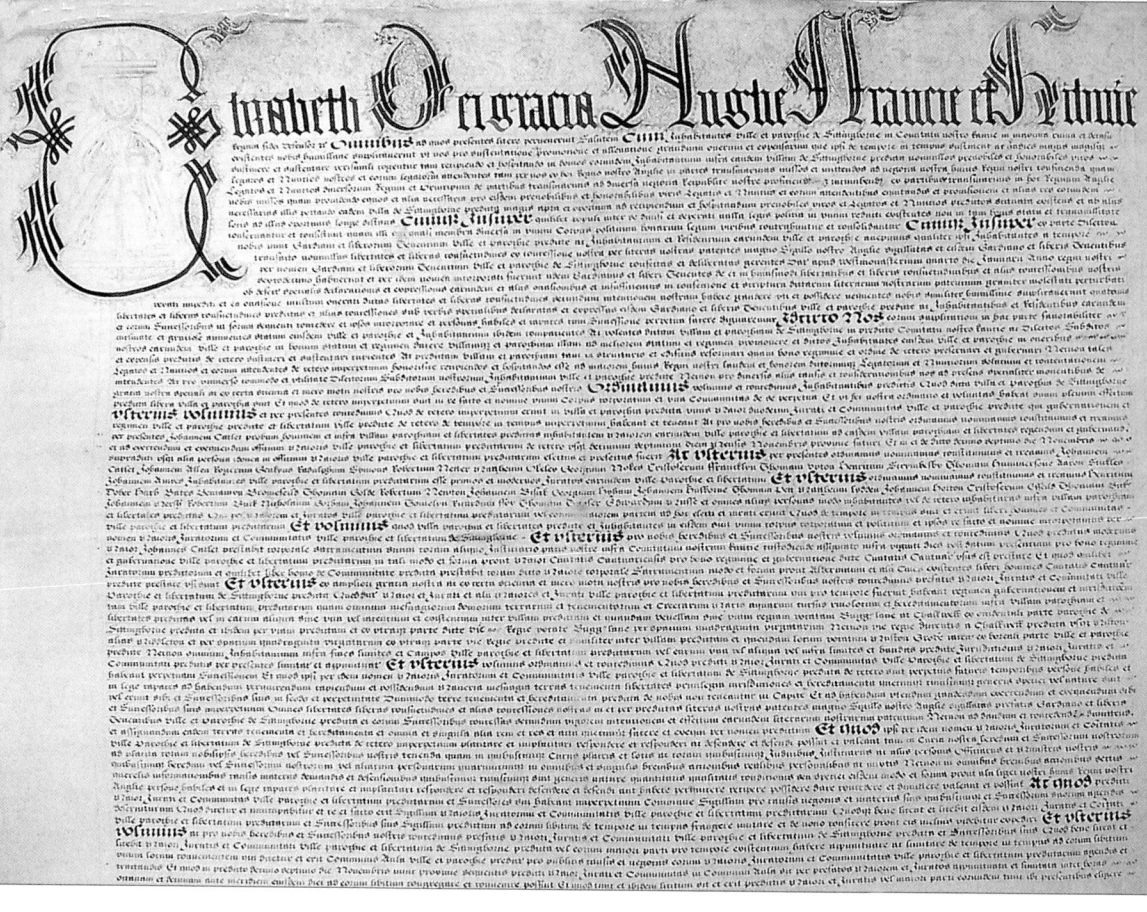

23 *A facsimile copy of Sittingbourne's second charter now hangs in the town's heritage museum. [Courtesy of Phil Talbot]*

by its situation, being at a convenient distance from other places … from the Warden and free tenants of the town … they may establish a corporation and create a perpetual succession of suitable and capable persons.

We do order … that the town and parish of Sittingbourne shall be a free town and parish and that henceforth, in perpetuity, there shall be one mayor, 12 jurats and a corporation which shall have and hold the government and guidance of the town.

We order John Catlet, an honourable gentleman, to be mayor of the inhabitants until the 17th day of November, until a suitable person shall be elected for the town. And further we order John Catlet, John Allen, Roger Genkyns, Randolph Symons, Robert Netter, Matthew Okeley, George Nokes, Christopher Ffranklyn, Thomas Upton, Henry Scrymbesby, Thomas Hummers, Aaron Stickles, and John Amyes to be the first jurats.

By the 16th century the economic relationship between Sittingbourne and Milton had undergone a radical change. Milton had become a major market and fishing port but, despite also being situated on the bank of the creek, with easy access to the Swale and its rich oyster beds, Sittingbourne had little involvement in fishing, even though it had two quays, one of which, 'Holeryche' or Holdredge, was mentioned in a will of this time. A register dated 1566, compiled in connection with the war with Scotland, records that Sittingbourne and Milton between them had 29 vessels, the largest being of 26 tons.

The differences between Sittingbourne and Milton continued to grow during the 17th and 18th centuries as Milton became a major fishing port, which dominated its economy, and the town became famous for its oysters, said to be on a par with those from Whitstable.

Royal patronage has long been a feature of Sittingbourne and this continued right up to the 19th century when Queen Victoria, as a young princess, together with Princess Leopoldine of Esterhazy, stayed at the *Rose*, occupying all of the first-floor rooms in 1825. In honour of the royal visit the hotel was renamed the *Rose and Victoria* for a short time. This former hotel, our last inn to rise to prominence, has been absorbed by Woolworth's and Clinton Cards; its tap house is now a Wimpy. Listed Grade II, it was built by a London merchant, Richard Jeffs, and the original inn sign is still embedded in the wall. The *Rose* was owned by Valentine Simpson in 1820 who also hired out post chaises and post coaches from 12s. 6d.

24 *Sittingbourne's last inn to rise to prominence was the* Rose *inn, premises now occupied by Woolworth's and Clinton Cards. [Courtesy of the Sittingbourne Heritage Museum]*

In looking back at the town's early character, it is interesting to see how the original buildings tended to be smaller than their modern counterparts, taking up less space within the plot. A classic example of this is the *Red Lion* public house, a relatively small medieval building on a north-south alignment, taking up only a portion of the whole site. The original building was enlarged with extensions, as the need arose, creating a courtyard at the centre of a block of accommodation and ancillary buildings. This section still survives intact and the north-south alignment of the *Red Lion* is itself an important feature. The burgage plots along the High Street were of a given size but were comparatively deep, allowing for a building to be constructed in such a way that allowed access to its rear from the High Street. Stables could then be built at the back of the building with access to the fields beyond for the horses. It was easier to build behind the main range than next to it as this land was already owned and in use by other parties.

Opposite the *Red Lion* once stood another couple of inns on the site where Brenchley House now stands. One, the *Crossed Keys*, has a most interesting past; it can also provide some insight into the history of the site, albeit indirectly. The name *Crossed Keys* indicates that this inn was an establishment owned and operated by the Church for pilgrims and those travelling on ecclesiastical business, like the craftsmen contracted to work on Church property. Such an inn would have been busy during the years of the pilgrimages but there would have been a decrease in trade when this started to die out, finally ending after the Reformation. This inn would then have been sold by the secular authorities who would also

have terminated the use of the name, yet it survived well into the 17th century. Could it be that the property was sold off before the Dissolution, during the period of decline in the pilgrimages? That way the inn could retain the name and, as the property was in private ownership, would not have been subject to the enforced changes by the secular authorities. The last known occupant of the *Crossed Keys* was 'Widow Mutton of Strood' during the Commonwealth period of 1640–60. As the site was still known as the *Crossed Keys* at this time, it can be assumed that the original medieval building was still standing and had been in private ownership since before the Reformation.

A Street of Inns
(Extracted from *Sittingbourne and the Names of Lands and Houses in or near it. Their Origin and History* by Canon Scott Robertson, published in 1879)

A virtual walk along the High Street, pointing out where some of our inns were once located. Starting at the Bull, an inn of long-standing, next to the entrance to Roman Square. Next door, to the west was the Horn, an early owner being John Norden in 1562. By 1820 it had become a private dwelling belonging to Edward Brenchley and occupied by William Castle, a surgeon. There was another inn squeezed in between the Bull and the Horn but that was absorbed into the premises of the Bull at an unknown date. Beyond the Horn lay two more inns, the Saracen's Head and the Gun. Both date back to at least 1562 and after being demolished, Brenchley House was built on the site. After ceasing to be an inn, the Saracen's Head became a private dwelling, while the Gun became the workhouse. By 1752 it was once again an inn, this time called the Globe, but it was not to last for long and soon reverted to being the workhouse once again. Eventually, when larger premises were found for the workhouse the old inn became part of a coachmaker's workshop.

Crossing to the north side of the High Street, the Six Bells stood between what is now Berry Street and the entrance to the Forum shopping Centre, formerly Crescent Street. In 1630 this inn had been known as the King's Head and from 1562-74 was owned by John Norden who also owned the Horn. Soon after 1752 it became a private dwelling, part of which became the workhouse. Between the King's Head and the Red Lion was once a forge but during the reign of George I it had been an inn, the Black Boy. Next came the Red Lion, to the east of which was the Boatswain's Call, adjacent to which was the Chequer, which ceased to be an inn some time prior to 1769. Following several changes in ownership, its easternmost portion became the taproom of the Rose, now Woolworth's and is now a Wimpy Bar. Beyond the Rose, built in 1708, stood the Swan. Next door to what is now Bateman's, opticians is a pet and garden shop that was once an inn, the Three Post Boys. After the Methodist church came the Bird in Hand, followed by the Fauken (Falcon?), an inn whose name in 1650 had been the Adam and Eve. The Fauken was built in 1562 but by 1769 had been extensively rebuilt as three separate private dwellings.

Moving back to the south side of the High Street, opposite St Michael's church was another group of inns. The first was the Angel, which by 1650 had

reverted to being a private dwelling and was demolished in 1735. Close by was the Portobello, popularly known as the Beggars' Opera but that too appears to have ceased trading by 1650. Further up the hill stands the George which dates back to c.1685.

Throughout the Middle Ages each parish was responsible for the care of its own poor, elderly, infirm and sick people and wills from this time show how benevolent the more affluent were towards their poorer neighbours. The parish took responsibility for costs incurred when people were taken ill or died as well as paying for young people's apprenticeships. Records show, for example, in 1676 John Elgate was paid £12 for taking Elizabeth Salmond as his apprentice with a further payment of 8s. 4d. for clothes for her.

Sittingbourne, like most medieval towns, once had alms houses, situated on the corner of East Street and Crown Quay Lane where Swale House now stands; its address is given as No.1 East Street. It accommodated eight poor widows and, although the original date of construction and by whom is no longer known, we know it was rebuilt in 1804. The almshouses were supported by several legacies including that of John Allen of Sittingbourne who left £2 p.a. in his will dated October 1615 for the repair and maintenance of the building and 'for firing for the poor inhabitants, to be made payable out of Glovers farm'. Likewise, Robert Hodsole bequeathed 10s. p.a. in his will of 1684, which was to be paid on Christmas Day to the poor out of Mrs Rondeau's land (Fairfield and Dark Orchard), and John Grant left £1 p.a. in his will dated November 1699 for the distribution of corn or bread, the money coming from Mrs Trott's farm. A more involved bequest was left by Katherine

Dicks in her will when she left £25 to be put in land security, 'the interest forever to be laid out in six twopenny loaves to be given to six poor widows who attended Divine service beginning on the first Sunday after Christmas Day'. In 1880 the principal was appropriated to church repairs at an interest rate of four per cent, payable out of rent of the Butts land, an acre of which, at the rear of the northern side of the High Street behind the Methodist church, was held by the churchwardens, and income from it was used for church repairs. The land was often used for fairs, etc. An unknown donor gave four seams (about 10 bushels) of boiling peas valued at about £12, which were to be distributed at Christmas.

Even as late as 1859 people were still bequeathing money to the alms houses and in December of that year John Huggens left £100. In 1877 George Smeed left £100 in his will 'to be invested in Consols for the purchase of bread to be distributed amongst the poor persons'. The provisions as to the appointment of the trustees of this charity by the urban district council did not apply until 1922. The power to appoint trustees of parochial charities under Section 14 of the Local Government Board Act, 1894 was conferred upon the council by order of the Local Government Board dated 17 June 1898.

Sittingbourne increasingly had to face the problem of more and more poor people coming here in the 18th century, perhaps lured by the prospect of plenty of agricultural work, so in 1722 a new system of poor relief came into force, which was still to be administered by the parish. Whereas the old system had been based on out-relief in which people were paid money and cared for in their own homes, the new system set up workhouses in which the poor were cared for and the

children educated. That early workhouse stood roughly to the east of Brenchley House in a former inn, the *Globe*, before later moving to where the shop Holland and Barrett now is. That building in earlier times had once been the *Kings Head*, later renamed the *Six Bells* and dated back to *c.*1630.

Life in the workhouse was both strict and harsh during the 19th century. The inmates were fed and clothed but in 1817 it was decided that their clothing would be identical, so when they went out they would become immediately identifiable. Some inmates went out to work each day as it was seen to be important that they were making an effort to help support themselves, and some of the children were educated at outside establishments, but woe betide anyone who had not returned by 6.30p.m.; they forfeited their supper. No-one went out after supper time. In times of acute unemployment it was not always possible to find work so in 1829, for example, it was decided that all able-bodied men seeking relief should be set to work as much as possible. When there was no work for them, they were encouraged to leave the area. By 1841 a fund had been set up to pay for them to emigrate to other countries.

A new life in a new land suddenly became a popular solution to local unemployment. We have records about two local people who took advantage of this new scheme and emigrated to America in the mid-19th century. In 1841 John Bridge received a letter from his brother-in-law who lived in Enfield, Connecticut. John lived in Milton and worked at the Faversham gunpowder works, to which he had to walk back and forth each day, so his brother-in-law wrote to tell him there was a gunpowder works in Enfield that was prepared to pay for John and his family to emigrate and to offer him a job. It was too good an opportunity to miss. Another known émigré was Caroline Brenchley, who had converted to the Mormon faith. After initially moving to London to work for the family of a doctor, she emigrated to Boston with them in 1856. There she left her employer and joined an ill-fated wagon train, the Martin Handcart Company. She was on her own as the wagon train struck out and she walked most of the way to Salt Lake City, the spiritual home of the Mormon faith. Having left Boston late in the year, the pioneers ran into exceptionally bad weather and many died en route. In 1859 Caroline married Thomas Obray, who had earlier converted her to the Mormon faith, and she became his third wife.

An enthusiastic campaign supporting emigration got under way and lectures were given at the Corn Exchange in 1870 pointing out the advantages of a new life in America. The local newspaper carried advertisements for books on 'Emigration for Poor Folks' and a letter from a mechanic who had emigrated to Canada was reprinted from the *Times* newspaper. By the mid-1880s emigration destinations had spread to Australia and Canada. Local emigrants often wrote home and in 1888 Alfred Goodhew, formerly from Milton, wrote a glowing report about his new life in Sacramento, California.

As unemployment increased in the years before the First World War, so too did the number of people wanting to emigrate. Special monthly services for those about to depart were held at St Michael's Church in 1911 and, in April of that year, 80 people, the largest ever party to leave Sittingbourne, departed for Canada and America. They occupied two complete carriages on the train from Sittingbourne and over a thousand people turned out to see them off. Their journey had been

arranged by the local travel agent, Hedley Peters. A popular destination was Oswego in New York State where there was a well-established group of people from Sittingbourne and Milton. Details of their births and deaths were often reported in our local newspaper. Another popular destination was Freemont, Ohio where again there was a large colony of former locals.

Some people continued to be supported outside the workhouse but in 1823 it was decided that, if these people kept a dog, they would lose their relief. Then, in 1833, the rules became even tougher when it was announced that the parish would stop paying for illegitimate children. To be receiving parish poor relief was a much-hated and despised stigma to most people. The parish finally relinquished its responsibility for the poor in 1834 when the Poor Law Act appointed local commissioners to organise unions and build new workhouses. If the old system was much feared and hated, worse was to come. All the poor, sick, elderly and infirm of Sittingbourne and the surrounding area that could not support themselves were sent to the new Milton Union in North Street, Milton Regis where life was made so unbearable that poverty could almost be seen as a crime.

Sittingbourne continued to be a thriving coaching centre, catering to the needs of travellers until the early 19th century when it entered a period of industrial development. The days of long, exhausting and sometimes dangerous travel by stage coach were numbered by 1858 when the railway came to Sittingbourne. London could now be reached in a matter of hours rather than days. The town's long-enjoyed position as an overnight resting place for travellers was no more. Some of the larger inns managed to stay in business but the majority failed and ceased trading; they were too small to meet the new demand. The coming of the railway brought a new breed of hostelry, public houses that sprang up around the station, offering refreshment and overnight accommodation to passing rail travellers. There is, for example, the *Fountain*, built in the mid-1860s, and the *Globe and Engine*, also built at the same time; prior to the construction of St Michael's Road there was a third one overlooking the station yard, the *Forester's Arms*. Pubs like these sprang up outside almost every railway station. The railway fostered the growth of Sittingbourne as an industrial centre and the expansion of the commercial functions of the High Street resulted in shops taking over buildings previously used as inns. An obvious indication of which shops were once inns is the presence of carriage archways still standing to one side. A couple of good examples are the *Rose*, a building now occupied by Woolworth's, and the *George*, our oldest inn, which was mentioned in a will dated 1478, but only the tap house remains to continue serving the public and has been renamed *The Entertainer*. The *Red Lion*, in a much-reduced form, still serves the town as a public house; the 'hotel' section later became a bank.

For much of its history the town's links between the urban and rural economies remained strong; Sittingbourne stands at the centre of a predominantly agricultural area but, following the demise of the stage and mail coaches, replaced by steam trains in 1858, the whole character of the town changed completely. It became one of Britain's leading centres for papermaking and brickmaking as all of its natural resources, including the creek, were brought together to great effect and Sittingbourne became a major industrial area of the South-East.

Chapter 4

Industrial Development

Until the 19th century Sittingbourne was surrounded by farmland, which had dominated the town's economy since the earliest of times. Agriculture was the main livelihood of the parish, employing nearly two-thirds of its population, despite also being a major contributor to the area's unemployment figures. Agricultural wages were so low, many workers simply could not afford to live on their income; it was not so for the farmers, who prospered. Close links between the Hundred and London developed as manure from the capital's stables and cattle markets was brought here to be spread on the fields and raw materials and farm produce sent back in return. An analysis of land use undertaken in 1992 showed that our agrarian economy had changed little since the 19th century or even earlier, but the 20th century was a period of rapid change typifying national changes in land use and agricultural trends. It could almost be likened to the period of the 16th-century Land Enclosures Acts. London no longer dominated our economy and the close agrarian relationship between urban and rural parishes had ended.

The beginning of the 19th century heralded a new direction and lifestyle for the people of Sittingbourne; the town was no longer a centre of hospitality for passing

25 *Dean's former jam factory in Bell Road, a sign of the region's surplus fruit production. These premises are currently occupied by Swale Housing Association. [Courtesy of the Sittingbourne library collection]*

travellers. The country's population was growing rapidly and it led to the start of three industries that were to shape Sittingbourne's future – brickmaking and cement manufacture, barge-building, and papermaking. By the middle of the 19th century, following the end of the Napoleonic Wars in 1815, the repeal of the Brick Tax in 1850 and an expansion of the railway network from the 1850s onwards, many of the villages around London started expanding to become suburbs of the metropolis. New buildings were constructed in the capital like the Law Courts, Tower Bridge, Kings Cross railway station, Westminster Cathedral and Buckingham Palace. The new railway routes themselves required a seemingly endless supply of bricks for their many stations, tunnels and bridges. The size of all these structures demanded an especially strong brick with a high tensile strength; the Kentish Stock brick was found to be ideal and Sittingbourne became its leading supplier. In his book *Stock Bricks of Swale,* Sydney Twist, a former brickmaker and leading authority on the history of brickmaking, maintains that he has never found the origins of the Stock brick, who discovered it or where it was first made, but feels sure it had to be in or near Sittingbourne in about 1700. The earliest-known Stock bricks Mr Twist has found were used in the construction of the *Rose* inn, now Woolworth's in the High Street, which was built in 1708. It was the town's location in a geologically perfect area, with large reserves of clay and chalk, the essential ingredients for brickmaking, and its location on the banks of the creek, giving easy access to the capital via a network of waterways, that played such a pivotal role.

Just as Sittingbourne had played a leading role in the 19th century by using London's large quantity of unwanted manure for agricultural purposes, so too did it by collecting the capital's refuse and ashes, an important ingredient in brick manufacture. An advertisement in a newspaper dated 1889 invited tenders for 'barges to carry away dust, ashes, garbage, refuse and street sweepings from the parish of Bermondsey for a period of twelve months, the estimated amount being 10,000 loads of dust and ashes and 9,000 loads of street sweepings'. It was an added bonus for the barges that took bricks and cement to London; rather than return empty they brought back a load of what was termed 'rough stuff'. It was a dangerous cargo to carry as there was an ever-present threat of spontaneous combustion and carbon dioxide fumes given off by the coke. Once unloaded, it was left in heaps on what became known as the Dung Wharf to rot down for up to a year, after which it was sorted, usually by women, pensioners and children too young for other work. The fine ash extracted from this heap was taken to be mixed with the brickearth and the coke was used to fire the clamps. Anything of value found during sorting was kept by the sorters as their perks.

Brickmaking was not a new skill; it had been introduced into Britain by the Romans and many examples of their bricks can be seen in the walls of most of our local churches. After the Romans left Britain in the fifth century the use of bricks went into decline until the 15th century but by the 16th century it had again become the accepted building material. The scale upon which the demand grew was enormous, leading to Sittingbourne becoming a brickmaking boom-town in the 19th and 20th centuries, employing over fifty per cent of the local workforce. Most of the brickfields were located in Murston and Milton but there were a few in what is now

26 *A section of the wall of Lower Halstow church showing how Roman brickwork was incorporated into the fabric of the building. [Mick Clancy]*

27 *A close-up view of the Roman bricks used in the construction of Lower Halstow church. [Mick Clancy]*

the town centre, places like the corner of Ufton Lane and West Street where the convent school was later built, Johnson House Gardens, College Road and Bassett Road, which explains their undulating terrain. The census returns for 1851 show that there were brickmakers and brick labourers living in Crown Quay brickfield so it's fair to assume there was a site there too, and in 1871 Henry Packham had a brickfield in what is now Valenciennes Road; it was small and closed down in about 1890. At this time the area south of the head of the creek was known as the old brickfield but the greatest concentration of brickmaking was undertaken in Murston where, later, cement was also manufactured.

By the end of the 19th century brickmaking was well established locally and it dominated our economy until well into the final decade of the 19th century. *Kelly's Directory* of 1895 confirms, 'The trade here is derived chiefly from the manufacture and transit of bricks and cement (nearly 6,000 hands being employed in these two industries)' – that's nearly forty-five per cent of the total 1891 population of Sittingbourne and district. *Kelly's* putting brick and cement manufacture first in its description of Sittingbourne is indicative of the changes taking place here in the second half of the 19th century. Thirty-three years earlier, in 1862, brickmaking had been mentioned almost at the end of the list of other trades and industries, which included 'the transit of passengers, the market, the supply of the neighbouring district, the shipping of corn and the import of coal'. Each of these continued to be undertaken in 1895 as they had done for centuries but by now they were greatly overshadowed by the area's 19th-century industrialisation.

Whereas the 19th-century expansion of London had led to the growth of Sittingbourne's brickmaking industry, changes in building policies and practice at the end of that century quickly eclipsed the golden age of the Stock brickmaking industry. Locally made bricks were of a high quality but were expensive to make. The new housing trusts and councils building in the capital's suburbs were not interested in the Stock brick's strength and durability. They wanted cheap bricks that were readily available from the continent. London's pollution had a chemical effect on Stock bricks, increasing their durability, but it also meant that many of its older buildings had become blackened and unattractive. The builders in the suburbs wanted red-faced bricks to set their houses apart from the older areas of the capital.

As demand fell and competition increased, the price of bricks plummeted, forcing a pay-cut for brickmakers in 1906. Local manufacturers faced the additional cost of Milton Conservancy Board's levy on goods coming into or out of the creek and, rather than helping to keep the creek open as a commercial waterway, it hastened its demise. Because of the levy, many smaller firms went bankrupt and the number of vessels using the waterway fell; gradually the creek became silted up and polluted.

Brickmaking lasted longer here than either of the other two industries, cement manufacture and barge-building, even though there were significant changes in production and the introduction of mechanisation in the 20th century, which led to a reduction in the workforce. All of

this took place in Murston as, by now, the smaller Sittingbourne brickfields, bar one, had long ceased production. That which continued in production until 1969 was Wills and Packham, whose brickfield lay to the north of the railway line where Eurolink Way now is. It can only be surmised that the reason why brickmaking continued for so long with expensive overheads was because of the heavy financial investment the manufacturers had made in mechanisation. By the early 1990s supplies of local brickearth were starting to run low and it seems unlikely that the industry will continue long into the 21st century. Whereas brickmaking once played such an important part in our local economy it is now a negligible contributor.

While much of our brickmaking history is attributed to George Smeed, another of our major producers, Daniel Wills of Wills & Packham, also made a valuable contribution to the town. Following a serious accident in his company's brickworks in 1898, he organised an appeal to raise money for the town's first public ambulance. A second ambulance was donated to the town by Mrs G.H. Dean in 1912. It was the first motor ambulance in Kent and was said to be the best in England.

Cement was being manufactured here on a small scale in the 1820s in a cement mill at Bayford where the original hamlet of Sittingbourne had once been. It was operated by Samuel and Charles Cleaver but in 1860 lightning struck the chimney and blew 30ft from the top of it. Six years later there was a fatal explosion and the engine house at the centre of the works was destroyed. John Huggens also owned a cement works at Crown Quay in the 1830s. The cement these two works produced was probably Roman cement rather than the

28   *The only tangible clue left as to the whereabouts of some of the smaller brickfields is that land levels are inexplicably different, as seen in this view of a field at Bapchild. [Mick Clancy]*

later-discovered Portland cement, which was produced in a totally different way. The main ingredient for Roman cement was septaria stone, found in the clay along the foreshore of the Swale. It was burnt in alternate layers with coal in a bottle kiln and, after cooling, was crushed into a fine powder in horse-driven crushing mills. Portland cement was manufactured using a mixture of chalk and mud, which was mixed in the wash mills and then drained off into decanting washbacks. This slurry was then dried before being layered with coal or coke in brick-built kilns. After it had been burnt, the cement clinker formed by the firing process was allowed to cool before being raked out and taken to the cement mill, where it was ground into a fine powder. Once sieved and graded it was packed into casks for shipment.

The coal used with the chalk/mud slurry was later replaced by gas coke, a cheaper alternative, following the development of the Sittingbourne Gas Works. A gasometer was erected in Crown Quay Lane in November 1863, providing gas lighting for streets and homes. This is another example of an interconnection between two industries.

The local cement-manufacturing industry continued to thrive throughout the 19th century, sending a considerable amount abroad, especially to the USA where the industry was just starting to develop, but by the early 1900s it had developed enough to become independent and Sittingbourne lost this valuable export market. The situation was further aggrieved when Belgium and Germany started to produce cheap, poor-quality cement that they exported to Britain. Our local cement works were not the only ones to suffer from the influx of cheap cement. Many of the smaller firms were forced to close while others amalgamated in 1900 to form the Associated Portland Cement Manufacturers, known locally as APCM. This consortium soon ranked among the most important cement manufacturers, controlling 80 per cent of the total Portland cement production outlets on the Rivers Thames and Medway. The Smeed Dean Cement Works located at Murston, which had been leased to the Burham Brick, Lime and Cement Co. (who joined APCM) in the 19th century, remained independent until 1924, something it was able to achieve because of the economic way in which the company was run. Its different but complementary business concerns helped it survive. This was pointed out in a cement industry report in 1901, which said '… it is not often bricks and cement are both manufactured by the same firm'. In the late 1920s Smeed Dean joined the remaining major independent cement manufacturers to form the Red Triangle Group; this consortium merged with APCM, by now known as Blue Circle, in 1931. On the downside of this merger, APCM brought in some of their own workers from other sites, making some Murston men redundant. But the greatest loss was not the manpower but the reduction in the size of the Smeed Dean barge fleet. Cement manufacture at Murston ended in the early 1970s on the grounds of economy as much as anything else. The Murston site had by now become

just a small part of a much larger operation centred at Northfleet; it was said that over 200 employees lost their jobs.

As the country's demand for more bricks and cement grew, our brickfields found that, although they could keep up with the demand, they needed larger vessels to transport them. And so the Thames spritsail sailing barge was born. They became the workhorse of water-borne transport and if the waterways can be described as the motorways of yesteryear, then the barges were certainly the juggernauts of their day. One of the largest barge owners on the creek was George Smeed who, with his partner George Hambrook Dean, owned around half of the Sittingbourne-based fleet, which at the time was upwards of 100 vessels. This highlights the dramatic growth of this industry; only 30 years earlier there had been just nine barges trading here. The local newspaper of the day suggested that there was probably no other creek in the kingdom that could boast of a similar amount of traffic than that of Milton Creek. Smeed saw the Thames spritsail sailing barge as the ideal vessel to carry bricks and cement into London. They were large, flat-bottom vessels with leeboards that made them ideal for use in shallow waters, needing only a 4ft draft and, despite their size, could be crewed by only two people. The 40ft mainmast and 30ft topmast could be lowered when approaching a bridge and their low, sleek design enabled them to slip under London's bridges with ease. Their basic design meant that they were relatively cheap to build using second-hand timber from the Royal Dockyards and, by skilfully combining the rig of a conventional coastal vessel with the hull design and leeboards of a small barge, Smeed found his barges could carry a large cargo into previously inaccessible

29   *Aerial view of the Smeed Dean works at Murston in the early 1920s.*

shallow draft ports, thus opening up new markets to him.

With so many creeks and inlets off the Swale, barge-building yards thrived; some were privately owned while others were owned by the brick and cement manufacturers. The number of barges trading from the creek continued to increase throughout the latter half of the 19th century and, while all are attributed to Milton, being the main port, the Mercantile Navy Lists show 190 were built in 1872, 343 in 1886 and 410 in 1900. Following APCM's takeover of the Murston works in the 1930s, most of Smeed Dean's barge fleet was sold off and

by the mid-1930s regular barge traffic to Murston had all but ceased. The barges were replaced initially by lighters and then, from the 1960s, by lorries. The sale of the Smeed Dean fleet of barges marked the end of an occupation that had played an important part in the town's economy for over seventy years.

Other large barge fleets were owned by brickmakers Wills and Packham, who had a fleet of 35 vessels known as 'teetotal barges', all named after notable Temperance reformers and bearing names like *Teetotaler, Band of Hope, Good Templar, et al*, each name being carefully chosen by Mr Wills. Wills and Packham built their

30   *Dolphin Sailing Barge Museum. [David Colthup]*

last barges on the creek between 1920 and 1922, the final one being the *Phoenician*. Local farmer and brickmaker Chas Burley also had a barge yard on the creek that in later years became the Dolphin Sailing

Barge Museum, named after the brand name of Burley's cement. Despite being a popular tourist attraction and a reminder of our once important role in the barge industry, in 2006 the landowner decided he needed the site for other purposes and the museum had to close down.

One of Sittingbourne's most notable barge-building families was the Taylors who in 1861 had a shipyard at Crown Quay. This was probably where John Huggens had previously had his cement works in the 1830s. Stephen Taylor, described as a barge-builder and ropemaker, employed 12 men and seven boys. Nearby, Taylor's sons, Stephen Jnr and John, also operated a shipyard. The census returns for 1871 show Stephen Jnr as a shipwright employing 14 workers while John, a shipbuilder, employed a similar number. Stephen's son George later became an engine-fitter while John's son Alfred followed in his father's

31   *Dolphin Sailing Barge Museum. [Picture by Barry Kinnersley]*

footsteps to become a boat-builder. By 1881 John Taylor and his family was the only surviving branch of the Taylors still engaged in the business, employing 12 men and four boys. Although barges were the main type of vessel built on the creek by the Taylors, they often diversified, such as in 1871 when they built a 200-ton schooner barge for a London-based owner and, more bizarrely, a floating swimming bath complete with a surrounding deck for changing rooms, to be located near Southend, built in 1881.

Another well-respected family of barge-builders was the Whites; the father had a yard at Sittingbourne while his son had yards at Conyer and Faversham. Between them they built many fine sailing barges. There was great rivalry between father and son as each tried to build a faster barge than the other. To settle matters a challenge race was organised between Mr White's *Victoria* and his son's *Satanita*. The race turned into a tragedy when a squall hit the *Victoria* and she capsized; both her owner Mr Austen and her skipper Capt. Webb were drowned.

The men who built the barges were proud of their work. They were master shipwrights who didn't work to drawings and plans but relied instead on their well-trained eye. All they would be given was the length, breadth and approximate tonnage of the proposed vessel. From this they would be expected to produce a half-model, which was carved from a solid block of wood with considerable accuracy. Very seldom was the finished product out by a ton or two. They were conscientious about every stage and aspect of the job no matter how large or small it might seem. They would fit a component of a new vessel, stand back and look long and hard at it, remove it, shave a bit more off, and once again stand back and scrutinise it. It

32   *After barges went out of use, many were driven ashore and left to rot on the banks of the creek and other water-ways. To this day it is still possible to pick out their remains in the mud at low tide as can be seen by this 1999 photo. [Mick Clancy]*

was only when the fitting looked perfectly alright to them that it was finally fitted in place. When it came to launch day they almost begrudgingly handed over 'their' barge to the riggers and painters. As a testament to how well Thames spritsail sailing barges were built at Sittingbourne, several regularly competed in sailing matches on both the Medway and the Thames. Of the 15 barges that took part

33 *The rotting remains of several of Sittingbourne's once proud barges can occasionally be found on the banks of the creek. 1999. [Mick Cl;ancy]*

in one race at Erith in 1864, seven had been built in Sittingbourne. Our highest-placed barge came second while the one single Sittingbourne-built stumpy barge came first in its race.

Working conditions in a 19th-century barge yard were primitive. Much of the work was done outdoors so the weather very much dictated the pace at which barges were built. If the weather was really bad, the workers were sent home and no work meant no pay. In extremely hot weather the timbers had to be kept covered with wood shavings to stop them warping and shrinking, which is why, later, large sheds were built over the sites. The 1890s day books from the Smeed Dean barge yard give a good insight into what life was like at the time and what sort of work was

being undertaken. In 1898 two barges were built. One cost £900 and the other £850. Other barges came in for repair and maintenance, some more often than others. The busiest months were between June and August, with an average of 23 vessels being repaired; the slackest period was December to February when the average fell to below ten. Some barges were laid up undergoing repair for several weeks with a number of jobs being undertaken on them, while others had a quicker turn around, needing only one straightforward job. Not all jobs were carried out at the yard; call-out was not unheard of. The barge *Conservation* was moored at Lower Halstow and needed a new tiller so workmen were dispatched there, charging the barge owner 3s. This was quite cheap as the average charge for repairs was £20. The yard's total income in 1898 was £2,300, which included the money received for building a new barge; the other barge was completed the following year.

The three industries, bricks, cement and shipbuilding came together in 1889 to support a common cause. Trade unionism was starting to grow and, following a strike in 1889 by London's dockers who won a pay rise, the Society for the Protection of Bargemen and Watermen was formed to protect its members' interests in future pay negotiations. The bargemen of Sittingbourne and Milton were among the first to join and formed Unity Lodge No.2 with between 400 and 500 members who were entitled to wear an anchor-shaped emblem on their watch chain and fly a special pennant bearing the initials BB at the masthead of their vessel. The lodge

was formed by the vicar of St Michael's Church, the Rev. Parry-Evans, who was the editor of *The Bargeman* magazine. It had a clubhouse in Crown Quay Lane, which was opened in 1921, on a piece of ground opposite the *Barge*, formerly the *White Hart* public house; the clubhouse was demolished in about 1942.

The success of the London dockers inspired Sittingbourne's bargemen to come out on strike against their poor pay structure, but it had a devastating effect upon the whole community. Brickworks owners could not afford to stockpile their bricks and had no alternative but to lock-out their workers. By the end of the second week the strike and lock-out had spread right along the Kent coastline with Sittingbourne at the centre of the dispute. In March 1889 over 5,000 brickies from Faversham, led by a brass band, marched in

34 *The* Cambria, *the last barge to trade in and out of the creek under sail. [Courtesy of the Cambria Trust]*

35   *A group of enthusiasts regularly spend their weekends bringing the* Cambria *back into ship-shape order. [Alan Cordell]*

procession to Sittingbourne and, together with others from Conyer, Murston, Sittingbourne and Milton, held a meeting, addressed by Mr Tookey, the vice-president of the Bargemen's Society, Mr W. Nicholls, a representative of the London Dock, Wharf and General Labourers Union, and Mr Cunningham-Gibson MP. It was an unbelievable demonstration of solidarity by brickies who had traditionally always been at odds with the bargemen. Three days later another procession of 3,000 workers paraded through the town carrying banners with slogans such as 'Stick like Bricks'. Solidarity was the order of the day and at this meeting it was agreed the bargemen would accept arbitration.

A relief committee was set up in Sittingbourne to organise soup kitchens but the strikers were reluctant to accept any help, seeing it as charity. They were proud men. By April 1889, with no sign of reconciliation, developments in other parts of the country started to cloud the issue. Brickmaking started to develop in Peterborough and because it had excellent rail links with London it gave real cause for concern that important markets for Sittingbourne's bricks would be lost.

Brickworks owners drew up a list of revised payments for carrying freight, claiming it represented a 10 per cent increase on the old rates, but the bargemen rejected it. An attempt was made to break the strike by two of Wills and Packham's barges sailing down the creek but they, and some of the Smeed Dean barges, were prevented from leaving by other vessels forming a barrier. Aboard one of the blocking barges was Mr Cole, Milton's portreeve, who defiantly read from the town's charter that he had the right to close the creek if he so wished. The strike finally came to an end at the end of April.

A slump in the brick trade during the first decade of the 20th century hit the bargemen badly. In reality they were earning less than they had in 1890. Action had to be taken and London dockers and watermen came out on strike. Local union members had to follow, although in fairness they were among the last to come out. They demanded higher wages and a 10-hour day. Not only did they get their demand of a 10-hour day but some workers also got a 6s. per week pay rise; others got considerably more. Such gains were not beneficial in the long run though as the barge industry continued to decline. The bargemen went on strike again in 1926, together with the brick and cement workers, this time for holidays with pay but on this occasion were not successful.

By 1946 sailing-barge traffic on the creek had virtually ceased but there was still cargo going in and out by tugs and lighters owned by papermakers Bowater Lloyd. The wooden lighters could carry up to 200 tons and their cargoes varied.

The third major industry to have an effect on Sittingbourne's 19th-century economy was papermaking, an industry that had been undertaken here since the early 18th century. Parish registers show there was a paper mill in Sittingbourne in 1737, owned by the Archer family. Unlike the later paper mills that used wood fibre as their raw ingredient, the early mills used rags, which were pounded into a mortar-like mix. By 1752 the mill was owned by William Stevens and was described as '… a paper mill, drying loft and rag house, newly built … and five acres of meadow land. The mill bays are newly repaired and there is always plenty of fine water and water carriage within a quarter of a mile of the mill.' It is clearly shown on a map dated 1769.

36 *To highlight their work restoring the* Cambria *members of the trust often give talks and hold exhibitions of barge memorabilia. [Alan Cordell]*

37   Part of an exhibition of barge memorabilia and artefacts given by Alan Cordell. [Alan Cordell]

By the early 19th century the mill was owned by Edward Smith, who must have been quite affluent as he had two servants. His address is given as Love Lane, later renamed Mill Street, Milton. Handmade paper later found in a solicitor's office bore the watermark 'E. Smith' and the Britannia double foolscap mark with the date 1820, which narrows down the period when Smith was making paper.

This industry was starting to grow by the middle of the 19th century and the census returns for 1841 show that there were 10 papermakers living in the same area as Edward Smith but he only continued until around 1850, after which the mill fell into disuse. The census returns of 1851 show just one former papermaker living in Milton.

There are several possible reasons why the mill fell into disuse. Smith might have tried progressing from making paper by hand to machine-made paper using a Fourdrinier machine, which was difficult to operate without highly skilled labour. It may equally have followed his actions to protect his machines. In 1858 a new road bridge was built over the head of the creek, which obstructed the mill's water supply. Smith ordered his workers to demolish the bridge and restore his water supply. There is a third possibility. In 1857 the East Kent Railway Bill was placed before Parliament and Smith lodged an objection on the grounds that if the line was built as proposed it would render his mill useless for papermaking as the smoke and dust from the trains would pollute it. This would suggest that Smith was still making paper by hand as it needs a clean atmosphere. The 1861 census returns offer no evidence of anyone making paper in either Sittingbourne or Milton.

The next owner of the Sittingbourne paper mill was Edward Lloyd who, for a

38 *Mill Street, formerly Love Lane, Milton Regis, once the home of 19th-century papermaker Edward Smith. The paper mill can be seen beyond. [Courtesy of the* East Kent Gazette*]*

number of years, had been making paper at Boxbridge on the River Lea just outside London. He specialised in manufacturing newsprint for his newspaper, *Lloyd's Weekly London Newspaper*, which he had started in 1842; it was succeeded by the *London Daily Chronicle* in 1876. Increasingly people were becoming literate and the last quarter of the 19th century saw the rise of the popular daily, a newspaper that required large quantities of newsprint. It was from the Sittingbourne mill that this demand was largely met. By 1863 Lloyd owned the Sittingbourne mill and the local newspaper spoke of '… three immense stacks of straw which stand high above Mr Lloyd's premises, formerly used as a paper mill'. The report went on to describe how 'the straw was of three kinds, and after it had been pressed into smaller compass by hydraulic power on the premises, it would be removed to the

mill at Bow'. It concluded by suggesting there was little probability the paper mill here would be put into working order and set in operation for some time to come.

Fire broke out on the site in August 1863, destroying most of the mill buildings, and it was not until 1866 that building work began on creating a new, larger mill, the basis of which we have today. Although sited near the old mill, the new mill was built nearer to the railway lines for convenience of transport. This shows that Lloyd was manufacturing a different sort of paper to Smith. It was anticipated the building works would take two years to complete but, once finished, Lloyd could expect to produce 50 tons of paper per week, compared to the output of just 36 tons from the Boxbridge mill. Once completed, a member of the Lloyd family came to take charge of the mill and in 1871 Edward Lloyd and his wife

39   *Aerial view of Lloyd's Paper Mill, c.1920.*

Mareanne moved into a grand house in Lloyds Square close to the mill. To begin with the mill operated on a small scale and was known as the *Daily Chronicle* Mills as Mr Lloyd owned the *Daily Chronicle* newspaper, which he purchased in 1876.

40   *The pump room bringing water into the mill.*

The census returns of 1871 show that, as well as Edward Lloyd, described as a 'paper mill overlooker', there were also six other paper mill workers, one printer and five labourers. Within 10 years the mill had grown considerably, according to the census returns of 1881; not only had the number of workmen increased but so too had the range of jobs they were undertaking. There were storekeepers, nightwatchmen, gatekeepers, stokers, engine fitters and engineers.

In 1877 G. & W. Bertram of Edinburgh erected the largest-ever papermaking machine at the Sittingbourne mill; it could produce 1,300 sq ft of paper per minute. Edward's son Frederick became manager and by 1882 the whole process had been transferred from Boxbridge to Sittingbourne.

To begin with most of the raw materials and the finished product were shipped in and out by barges that tied up at the nearby creek. The mill was connected to

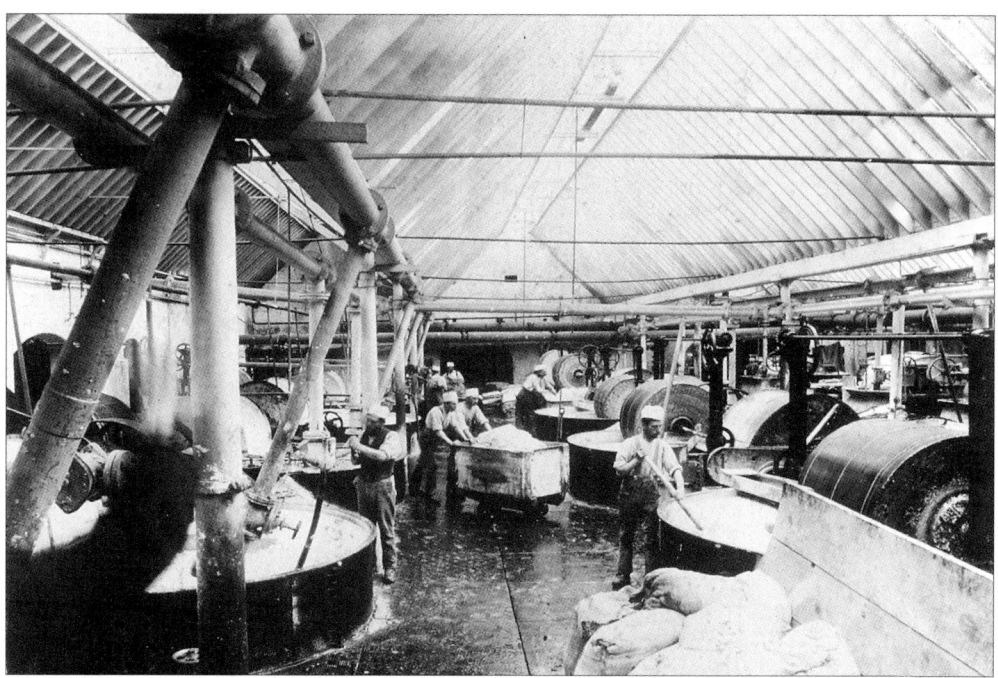

41 *One of the many stages in papermaking.*

the quay by a horse-drawn tramway. It was not until 1906 that this was replaced by a steam train.

With such a volatile product and ingredients, fire was an ever-present threat. In 1883, 300-400 reels, each containing four-to-five miles of paper, caught fire and were destroyed. The huge stockpiles of straw and esparto grass often caught fire. Straw and esparto grass were found to be an ideal substitute for rags, which had been in short supply after 1860. The esparto grass was imported from Spain where Lloyd held the right to cut huge areas of land.

The size of the mill and its machinery continued to expand throughout the latter decades of the 19th century and into the 20th century. Its workforce also grew in size and by 1891 it employed over 140 people. In January 1890 Edward Lloyd Ltd became a limited liability company with a capital of £250,000.

Unlike the brick and cement manufacturing industries, which had faced problems in the early part of the 20th century, the papermaking industry entered a period of growth, due in no small way to

42 *The finished product.*

43 *Stoking the mill's boilers was a never-ending job.*

44 *Millworkers checking the paper as it moves through the machines.*

the efforts of Edward and his son Frank who continued being at the forefront of new developments. For example, in the 1890s they installed what was, at that time, the widest papermaking machine in England. It was the fastest then being used and had an output of 50 tons of paper per week. Ever conscious about obtaining plentiful supplies of raw materials, the Lloyds bought up large areas of land in Algeria and Spain, where they secured the rights to cut esparto grass. They were also one of the first paper manufacturers to use wood pulp as a raw material and bought a pulp mill in Norway to supply it. Just as George Smeed had diversified to succeed in the brick and cement manufacturing industries, so too did Edward Lloyd. In 1913 work began on a dock for ocean-going vessels weighing up to 3,500 tons at Ridham on the Swale near Kingsferry Bridge. It was connected to the

Sittingbourne mill by a light-gauge steam railway, a timely move as by now the creek was gradually silting up and no vessels of any significant size could get anywhere near the mill.

In 1910 United Newspapers Ltd, with Edward Lloyd Jnr as director, was formed to buy Lloyd's newspapers, thus keeping them separate from the papermaking side of the business. The Sittingbourne mill was by now the largest of its kind in the world. The company's capital amounted to £1,270,000, making it the largest papermaking business the industry had ever seen.

Following the death of Edward Lloyd Snr in 1890, his son Frank assumed control of the mill. He sold off the company's newspaper interests to United Newspapers in 1918 and concentrated on papermaking. Part of the sell-out contract

45 *Lloyd's Paper Mill, c.1907.*

46   *Millworkers checking the paper at the end of its manufacturing process.*

47   *A rear view of the mill.*

48   *Hard at work in the machine shop.*

was that United Newspapers would buy all their newsprint from Lloyd's for a period of 30 years from 1920.

As production increased in the early 20th century, more water was needed. At first the stream that flowed down Ufton Lane and Cockleshell Walk en route to the creek was more than adequate but it quickly dried up. The company bored wells into the subterranean reservoir beneath the Meads at Milton and piped the water into the mill; it was also later piped to the new mill at Kemsley.

Lloyd's continued their innovative and ground-breaking work for a number of years. Accidents were commonplace in the mill and Sittingbourne did not have a hospital where serious cases could be treated. In 1911 it was suggested in the local newspaper that an application be made to the King Edward VII Memorial Fund for money to build a small cottage hospital but when it opened in 1930 the memorial hospital in Bell Road was not in memory of the king but of Mrs Frank Lloyd; it was a gift to the town from Mr Frank Lloyd and his daughter. Lloyd's set up a medical insurance scheme for their workers, who paid 1d. per week into it. The company also built a social club in the Avenue of Remembrance and a well-appointed sports ground in Gore Court Road, both which are still used by papermakers and others to this day. They even made generous donations towards the building costs of the old public swimming baths

49   *Lloyd's Social Club in the Avenue of Remembrance.*

that once stood in the Butts and Trinity Hall, off Dover Street. Like brickmaker George Smeed, the Lloyd family were true benefactors of Sittingbourne.

A shortage of wood pulp and an increased demand for paper in the 1920s led to a rapid price increase and, despite the introduction of a three-shift system in 1919, which became the mill's accepted work pattern, the demand exceeded the mill's capacity. With no more room to expand, the company purchased land at Kemsley and in 1923 started to build their second mill. Like that at Sittingbourne, it too was connected to Ridham Dock by the company's own railway line but Kemsley also had an aerial steel ropeway transporting logs from the dock directly into the mill. With the new mill came a

new village for its workers, called Kemsley. Frank Lloyd was clearly influenced in his plans for it by the development of other new garden towns and cities built elsewhere at this time.

Frank Lloyd died in 1927, leaving no designated successor, so following his death the business was sold to Berry's, the owners of Allied Newspapers, for £3.2m. In announcing the buy-out, Sir William Berry told his shareholders that the Sittingbourne and Kemsley mills between them were the largest in the country, larger even than any in Canada or the USA, with an annual output of some 200,000 tons of newsprint. Under its new ownership expansion continued into the 1930s but continuing economic depression, together with increasing overseas competition,

50   *Aerial view of Kemsley Paper Mill. In the bottom-left corner can be seen the much-disputed site of Castle Rough.*

51   *Aerial view of Ridham Dock on the banks of the Swale.*

especially from Canada, made newsprint production less profitable. In 1936 the mills were sold to Bowater's. Such was the size of the company by then, many thought it was the Sittingbourne and Kemsley mills taking over Bowater's. Together they employed over 3,000 workers and were producing on average 6,500 tons of paper per week. Bowater Lloyd became the largest newsprint producers in Europe, being responsible for 60 per cent of Britain's total output.

Throughout the Second World War and the years immediately after, although the demand for newsprint was greatly reduced, the company was able to adapt to other needs for the war effort. The company became Bowater Lloyd Pulp and Paper Mills Ltd in September 1948 and in 1955 changed to Bowater's United Kingdom Pulp and Paper Mills Ltd. As the years rolled

on into the 1950s and 1960s, production started steadily to pick up once again. But as computerised operated machinery and new working practices were gradually introduced, workers started to be laid off. It began when 'time and motion' experts recommended replacing the railway with road transport; it was closed down in the autumn of 1969. It all came to a head in 1980 when, by then, the workforce had dropped to just eight hundred. Bowater's sold the Sittingbourne mill to New Zealand firm Fletcher Challenge. The old mill was being used by the Sittingbourne Paper Company, part of UK Paper. In 1992, with a national and international recession affecting the paper industry, Fletcher Challenge announced the closure of part of Sittingbourne's packaging plant with the loss of 100 jobs. The role of the

52   *The offices of Lloyd's Paper Mill, c.1920. What fine architecture for an industrial site.*

paper mill within our local economy had declined and the town was no longer reliant on its last remaining major industry. Finnish paper manufacturers M-real took over the running of the mill in 1999 but at the end of 2006 announced that it would be closing its Sittingbourne mill in 2007 due to rising costs and a falling demand for paper.

The mill has left a lasting legacy of its past, part of the narrow-gauge light railway that once connected the Sittingbourne and Kemsley mills to Ridham Dock. The line was opened in 1906 to transport wood pulp and coal to the Sittingbourne mill from the creek but in an effort to improve upon efficiency a dock was built at Ridham near Kingsferry Bridge. The First World War interrupted building works and the Admiralty commandeered the site for a

53   *A paper mill is not the most glamorous of settings for a moonlit shot – or is it?*

salvage depot with a standard-gauge railway line linking it to the Sheerness branch line. It was handed back in 1919 and the line to Sittingbourne was built. Kemsley mill was

54   *The paper mill as seen in 1999. [Barry Kinnersley]*

55 *A former paper-packing shed shortly before demolition, 1998. [Barry Kinnersley]*

built in 1924 and it too was linked to Ridham Dock by the railway line. It was a useful and time-saving way of transporting men and materials between the three sites until it closed in 1969, when Bowaters decided it was no longer economical to keep the line open.

Fortunately, the company was far-sighted enough not to abandon totally the line and tear it up. Instead they offered the section from Sittingbourne to Kemsley to the Association of Railway Preservation Societies, who, in turn, approached the Locomotive Club of Great Britain in October 1969, who in 1971 passed the lease on to the Sittingbourne and Kemsley Light Railway Ltd. Since then it has been run as a highly successful and popular tourist attraction. Amazingly, two of the original locomotives, *Premier* and *Leader*, are still in service.

As beneficial as the paper mill had been to the town's economy, it was not without its downside. The mill was responsible for much of the pollution experienced around it. As long ago as 1878 people living near the mill expressed their concerns about the smoke, fine ash and sulphuric fumes belching from its chimneys. By 1892, with no improvements having been made, the people again protested to the mill owners

56 *The terminus of the Sittingbourne & Kemsley Light Railway, once an industrial railway but now a popular tourist attraction. [East Kent Gazette]*

about the nuisance. Lloyd's blamed the inferior quality coal they were being forced to use due to a coal crisis in the North of England. The mill was also accused of polluting the creek. The problem first came to light in 1895 but, despite the Milton Creek Conservancy Board being set up to manage and control the use of this busy waterway, the problem persisted. It got so bad, when the tide was low and the wind was in the east, that a sulphuric smell resembling bad eggs swept across the whole town and sometimes beyond. It was said that the creek was the worst-polluted area in the South of England. A campaign was started in the mid-1960s to get rid of the awful smell and in 1974 a survey by P.M. Bailey won him a National Environment competition.

In all fairness, the paper mill was not entirely to blame. With the steady decline in the number of vessels using the creek and with no fast-flowing streams to purge it, the waterway was gradually silting up. Layers of pollutants had built up to six

57 *A Sittingbourne & Kemsley Railway steam train in its former commercial role transporting bales of paper. [Chris Deamer]*

inches deep and had the texture of soggy cardboard. These suspended solids were deposited along the banks of the creek, and encroached on the main channel. Areas constantly washed by the tides quickly became coated in a thick, greasy, corrosive deposit. The mill owners made

58 *Three 'S & K' steam engines load up with water before the start of the day's work. [Chris Deamer]*

59 *A selection of exhibits in the former Dolphin Barge Museum. [Barry Kinnersley]*

second half of the 19th century. The decline in the town's earlier role as a centre of hospitality was linked not so much to the growth of these industries, but to changes in transport methods. The railway had arrived in Sittingbourne, making London accessible in a matter of hours. The brickmaking boom came just in time to save the town's economy. Much of Sittingbourne High Street is now a conservation area, protecting what little remains of our once-glorious past, but sadly the same cannot be said of the brickfields, of which little now remains. In the 1970s our vast creek-side industrial landscape became a sea of industrial estates and, by way of a tribute to the former brickmaking industry, the developers built two decorative kilns in Eurolink Way. To me they look more like the bottle kilns more usually associated with the potteries industry rather than the brick kilns I remember! Only one former barge yard, Burley's, remained and that became the Dolphin Sailing Barge Museum but in 2005 the landowner announced

considerable efforts to stop the pollution and by 1991 had spent over £4m to meet new European Union targets to clean up the discharged water.

These three industries between them changed the face of Sittingbourne completely and irrevocably during the

60 *When Milton Congregational Church was demolished a number of headstones of significant barge people were found in its graveyard. They were dug up and placed at the back of the Dolphin Barge Museum for safe keeping. The corpses were re-interred in a mass grave in Sittingbourne cemetery. [Barry Kinnersley]*

61   *Adelaide Dock, Murston, c.1930, once a major quay for exporting bricks and cement.*

62   *George Smeed owned the most impressive house, the 17th-century mansion, Gore Court. After its demolition the land upon which it stood was given to the townspeople for use as a playing field, known today as King George's Playing Field. The stable block and coach house remain as a café; changing rooms and a function hall and traces of the columns that once supported the portico can still be found.*

63 *Brickmaker Daniel Wills built a fine town house, Garfield House in Park Road, complete with a lofty tower from where, it is said, he could keep his eye on his barges entering and leaving the creek.*

he had other plans for the site and gave the museum notice to quit. The museum had operated in the former sail loft and forge since about 1969, when a group of barge enthusiasts set about transforming the derelict site into a working museum. It was opened by Cllr Brian Buckey in 1970 and took its name from the brand name of cement formerly made at Burley's cement works. After only a few years the museum was forced to close down due to operational difficulties but by 1978–9 a group of London-based barge enthusiasts, together with some knowledgeable barge owners, reorganised and reopened the museum. This time it was opened by Col. Donald Dean VC, who, as a descendant of brickmaker George Hambrook Dean, had had a barge named after him, the *Donald*. After Col. Dean won his gallantry award in the First World War the barge was renamed the *VC*. The museum became a popular local tourist attraction, especially among schoolchildren, and was the only one of its kind in the South-East. The museum buildings consisting of the sail loft and forge are two of the original buildings and their future at the time of writing is uncertain. Today there are no tangible links left of this once-busy industry.

64 *Could Daniel Wills see his barges from the top of his lofty tower? I put this myth to the test and, despite an extensive 20th-century urban sprawl, it does not seem likely. It is difficult even to see the creek itself. [Barry Kinnersley]*

Chapter 5

Later Urban Growth

For many years Sittingbourne was administered, firstly by the Vestry (representatives of the parish who met in the church vestry), and later by a mayor and 12 elected jurats, or councillors, as decreed by the charter of 1599. But by the 19th century, following a period of rapid expansion, great changes started to take place; Sittingbourne had become a recognised town. From 1874 the town was administered by the Sittingbourne Urban Sanitary District Authority, which was succeeded by Sittingbourne Urban District Council under the Local Government Act of 1894. This continued until the Kent (Sittingbourne and Milton) Confirmation Order (1929) amalgamated it with Milton Council to form Sittingbourne and Milton Urban District Council, which continued until local government reorganisation in 1974 when it became Swale Borough Council. An attempt to amalgamate Sittingbourne and Milton was first made in 1902 but it failed in the face of a staunch campaign to 'Keep Milton for the Miltonians'. The motion was defeated by 783 votes in favour of the amalgamation and 1,384 against it; Milton had a long history of wanting to remain independent and keep its ancient privileges. In November 1907 it was granted permission to add the suffix 'Regis' to its name in recognition of its past royal connections and to differentiate it from similarly named towns at Gravesend and Canterbury. To avoid mail going astray people had come to refer to the town as 'Milton-next-Sittingbourne'.

The amalgamation of 1929 had many points in its favour. Although the two towns had each once had separate identities, as they gradually expanded their boundaries these had become blurred and they now constituted one town. The way the boundary crossed over streets and through houses caused significant problems, not least in the supply of water and sewage disposal. Some streets had two or more sewers and water mains, and both towns went to considerable expense to pump sewage to their respective sewage treatment works, which could without cost easily drain into one another. Furthermore, it was uneconomical to have two town halls, two fire brigades etc when one would suffice. It was a situation fraught with problems. For example, in 1872 a fire engine arrived at an incident and found its hose did not fit the water hydrant. By amalgamating, the two towns would acquire greater status than they each had alone. Even though both towns had their own populations, all the public amenities were located in Sittingbourne. Amalgamation made perfect sense. Finally, in 1929, it was agreed that the two towns, together with Murston, would amalgamate but the suggestion that the new authority should be known as Milton and Sittingbourne UDC was rejected; it was to be Sittingbourne and Milton. Five years later Milton Regis lost its rural district council when it was amalgamated with Faversham RDC to form Swale RDC.

This ludicrous situation was highlighted by an amusing comment in the *East Kent Gazette* newspaper following the 1931 national census, which showed that Sittingbourne had 10,087 males and

65   *Sittingbourne Fire Brigade in the early 1900s.*

10,088 females. It said '... the town has two town halls, two fire brigades, two waterworks, two surveyors BUT only *one* surplus woman; rumour has it she has emigrated'!

Another official local body was the Milton Union (which included Sittingbourne) that was set up in 1835 to look after the poor, the destitute, the homeless and the elderly, and continued until 1930 when it amalgamated with the Faversham and District Guardians Committee, which carried on until 1948 and the formation of the National Health Service; it ran in parallel with the town council.

By the mid-19th century Milton was still the larger of the two towns and was expanding rapidly; it was then that many of our interconnecting roads and streets were built. A contributing factor to the growth of the two towns was the arrival of the railway in November 1857. Station Street, then known as Station Road, was built in 1860 to connect the High Street to the railway station, followed by The Wall, connecting Milton to Sittingbourne; it was said to be the darkest and dirtiest road in town. This is not surprising as it closely follows the boundary wall of the paper mill, hence its name. In 1864, a 41-acre plot was purchased from Capt. Vallance, which ran from the High Street southwards to the top end of Tunstall Road, now Ufton Lane. It was named Park Road and, in 1869, it and the nearby William Street and Eastbourne Street were adopted by Sittingbourne Council. In the

66   *For over four decades Sittingbourne fire brigade was headed by Hedley Peters senior, followed by his son of the same name. Here he stands with the crew with the new Shand Mason appliance in 1898. It was christened Victoria and cost £220.*

same year, the British Land Company Ltd asked the council to take responsibility for Shortlands Road, Milton Road, Cooper Street, Harold Road, Goodnestone Road and Shakespeare Street but only Shakespeare Street was accepted. Taking on the responsibility to maintain roads, paths and drainage was expensive. For example, in 1869 the Sittingbourne Improvement Commissioners had to dispose of a build-up of water beneath the railway arch in Milton Road because in the winter the road became almost impassable. To solve the problem the commissioners had to cut away the hillside, lower the end of the road and underpin the shops and houses so that the water could drain away to the nearby reed pond. The work cost over £100.

By 1881 there were 28 more streets in the town. Some of the long-established street names were changed and street-name plates began to appear at the corners of each street. It was then decided that there would be no more streets called terraces

so Lloyd's Terrace became Lloyd Street and Albion Terrace and Malcomb Place became part of Canterbury Street, now Road. 1891 saw the start of a development known as the Rock Estate, south of the

67   *Station Street, 1974. [Fred Atkins]*

68 *The Wall, Milton Regis, 2007. This road was once said to be the filthiest, darkest and most disease-ridden street in Sittingbourne, a reputation no doubt earned by its closeness to the boundary wall of the paper mill. When this wall was built, six streets were lost. [Barry Kinnersley]*

London Road. Once complete it gave the town Rock Road, Burley Road and Epps Road. Prior to the start of building work, this patch of land had formerly been a favourite place for trade unionists to hold their meetings.

As the urban area continued to grow, more streets and more houses developed; the need for more housing was getting acute and overcrowding was rife. In 1925 the housing inspector reported that, of the 1,965 houses in the area, 237 had two or more families living in them. One answer was for the council to support the owner-occupier scheme under which the council granted a subsidy of £75 per house and an advance of 90 per cent of the valuation of a house. This they believed would encourage people to build new houses and reduce overcrowding without the need for the council to have to build new houses themselves. By 1927 'model villas' were being advertised in Ufton Lane and Rock Road.

The scheme had some success and houses in Glovers Crescent and Trotts Hall Gardens were sold to tenants. The South Avenue Housing Estate was built by the council in 1930, the first houses to be built here with electric lighting, and in the following decades house building continued apace until the late 1940s/early 1950s when the council completed its building programme with the Homewood

69 *The High Street, c.1911.*

70 *The High Street featuring the* George *in the early 1900s.*

71   *The High Street looking towards St Michael's Church in the early 1900s.*

Avenue, Canterbury Road and the North Court estates.

Other local roads of note built at this time include Bell Road, which was transformed from a narrow hedge-lined lane into a desirable residential road; Cromers Road, which replaced an old bridle path, and the Avenue of Remembrance, a war memorial dedicated to those who were killed in the First World War and built under the unemployment relief scheme.

With the arrival of the railway in Sittingbourne and a complete change in the town's economy, a meeting was held to consider establishing a corn market here. The meeting was held in public rooms in Crescent Street, where the entrance to the Forum Shopping Centre now is; it was chaired by Mr Eley of Tonge. Mr Gordelier, who owned the public rooms, suggested that his premises were ideally located and could be extended if necessary.

They were close to the High Street and near the bank. However, Mr Lake pointed out that, if the building was used, Mr Gordelier would suffer financially in the long term but, even so, the building gave no attraction to the town. A new building would be the best option and Mr Knight of Bobbing proposed that it should be built near the railway station. Mr Dean objected to this, pointing out properties situated near railway stations were of little value in most towns, so he suggested that a High Street site in the town centre, on the corner of what is now Central Avenue, would be more beneficial. The meeting agreed to this and in 1858 tenders for the new building were requested. The lowest came in at £1,090 16s. 3d. and the work commenced; William Lake laid the foundation stone in August 1858. The shareholders decided market day would be on Wednesdays, the first being 12 January 1859.

72   *The corner of Bell Road, High Street, Crown Quay Lane and East Street where it is conjectured the early town started to grow, c.1920.*

73   *Crescent Street school rooms, the site of the earlier public rooms where the decision to build a corn exchange was taken in the closing decades of the 1800s. This view was taken in 1972 before Crescent Street was demolished to make way for the entrance to the Forum shopping centre. [Fred Atkins]*

Sittingbourne Corn Exchange was officially opened on 25 January 1859 with a grand concert, but a couple of weeks earlier it had been acoustically tested when a lecture was held in the hall to dispel the fear that '… the lofty pitch of the Corn Exchange would cause unpleasant reverberation or echo'. The only drawback in the design was found to be an uncomfortable draught due to the doors not closing properly. The following year the outside of the building was embellished by the addition of a triple-dial clock set in a cupola.

In 1878 the Corn Exchange was taken over by the Sittingbourne Urban Sanitary Authority and after improvements had been made it was reopened as the town hall wherein they held their meetings. Urgent repairs were needed in 1894 when a large section of the ceiling collapsed.

Even though it never housed any of the council's departments, the town hall was used extensively for council meetings, concerts, exhibitions, dances, etc right up to its closure and demolition in 1965.

The town was rapidly growing in size and in 1860 the local newspaper published a letter from a reader who described Sittingbourne as '… past praying for, a sink of abominations, reeking with impurities, a very hot-bed of disease, and where the inhabitants are so sunk in squalor, as to be walking about merely to save the burial fees'. As horses were the main form of transport and the town had no sewage system or clean water supply, this is probably an accurate picture of the town at that time. The newspaper called for '… proof that the heaps of offal and vegetable matter, the black pools and stagnant gutters, in the midst of which our fellow townsmen eat,

74   *The old town hall in the High Street.*

75 *The High Street, looking westward.*

drink and lie down, as claimed in the letter, actually existed'. Obviously nuisances did exist and in 1865 it was pointed out to the newspaper that there were two or three piggeries in the town where barrels of stale blood and piles of manure could be found within a few yards of houses tenanted by respectable people. Given such living conditions, it is not surprising that disease was rife. There was an outbreak of cholera in East Street in 1866. A blackspot for fever of a severe and typhoid-like character was The Wall in Milton, on the banks of the head of the creek. There were more reported cases here than in the rest of the town. Clearly something had to be done to improve matters.

The first problem to be addressed was the provision of a clean water supply. For too long the townspeople had drawn their supply from the highly polluted creek and wells in their back gardens. In 1870 pipework was laid from Keycol Hill waterworks into the town. There was still no adequate sewage system and the new water supply may have had an adverse effect on the health of residents in some cases. It was said in some areas that, once the houses had piped water, the residents used their former well as a cesspit, which contaminated other wells with sewage, thus increasing the likelihood of cholera. For example, the houses in William Street did not have piped water, relying instead on wells that became unusable when the houses in nearby Park Road had piped water installed and the residents began to use their old wells as cesspits. The sewage totally contaminated the underground supply.

It was suggested in 1870 that Sittingbourne and Milton should amalgamate to form a single body to deal with sanitary requirements. The two towns were almost conjoined so it made perfect sense. At first Milton bought its supply from Sittingbourne, whose waterworks were at Keycol Hill but by 1879 Milton demanded an equal share in running the waterworks; Sittingbourne would not agree to this. A commission of the Local Government Board was instigated to look into the dispute and it concluded that the three local boards, Sittingbourne, Milton and Rural, should be kept separate. Sittingbourne was given control of the Keycol Hill waterworks and Milton was to pay half the cost of building the plant and laying the mains to the junction with their pipes, plus a third of the annual working expenses in return for the right to a water supply in perpetuity. In 1896 the waterworks was enlarged but differences between the two authorities continued and in 1899 Milton Council refused to meet Sittingbourne Council to discuss the question of water supply and sewage disposal. Instead, Milton built its own waterworks at Highsted in 1906; Sittingbourne had, meanwhile, opened a sewage treatment works in 1904. It would not be until the 1930s that the water supply and sewage disposal issue between the two towns was finally resolved when the two councils were amalgamated. The Highsted and Keycol Hill waterworks were then linked in 1932, the Highsted works were improved in 1938 and a new joint sewage works was opened in 1934. Most

of the earlier problems over sanitation and water supply between Sittingbourne and Milton had been overcome by the mid-20th century and the Church Marshes sewage treatment works were extended in 1972.

As more and more roads and streets with their associated houses were built and the population steadily increased, the churchyard of St Michael's Church quickly started running out of space for new burials. A piece of land in Bell Road was purchased for £600 and in 1860 the Burial Board decided to build a mortuary and chapel on it at a cost of £1,430. It opened for business in October 1860, offering 9ft by 4ft graves for £1 in perpetuity, £4 for a 9ft by 8ft vault, 7s. 6d. for digging and filling an adult grave, 10s. 6d. for erecting a headstone and 1s. for tolling a bell at a funeral. The fees were doubled if the burial was of a non-resident of the town.

Another offshoot of the population explosion was a demand for public open spaces for leisure-time pursuits. The Albany Road recreation ground was purchased for £2,200 in 1879; the grass and fencing cost a further £700.

Improvements were made to the postal system and in 1870 Sittingbourne's post office was connected to the telegraph system. Messages still continued being received at the railway station and it was not until 1879 that there was a direct link between the post office and London. A new sub-post office was opened in East Street in 1885 and in 1892 a new main post office was opened in the High Street. The premises next to the *Bull*, which had been in use for 15 years, had become too small so a former outfitters' shop further down the High Street where Blundell's furnishers, the old *George Hotel*, now stands was converted. It became a state-of-the-art post office with a long polished mahogany counter and a post box inside as well as outside. The system for handling money orders was improved and, after telegram messages had been written, they were carried to the upstairs office in a small lift. The sorting office behind the main room employed up to eight sorters and upstairs, as well as the telegraph office, there was a room for the local inland revenue officer as well as a flat for the caretaker and his family. It was said to be one of the most complete post offices in Kent and, according to the local newspaper, it lacked only one essential item, a gas lamp outside to highlight the building's importance. The post office remained here until 1911 when it moved to premises near the Baptist Church, formerly the home of surgeon

F. Grayling, and which older residents will no doubt remember. It moved to Central Avenue in 1961.

An interesting piece of information came to light when Bryan Clark of the Historical Research Group of Sittingbourne discovered an intriguing tombstone in St Michael's churchyard. It read 'Sacred to the memory of George Sargent, postman of this Parish, twenty six years, who departed this life 19th December 1849 age 57 years, also Elizabeth wife of the above who died 10 March.' The rest of the epitaph was not legible, but Mr Clark later found that Elizabeth had died in 1833, aged thirty-eight. In further researches Mr Clark could not find a birth or marriage certificate in

76   *The old post office standing where today there is Argos.*

77   *The High Street looking westwards with the old Post Office to the left.*

the Sittingbourne parish registers, but did find three children baptised of a George and Elizabeth Sargeant; there was no mention of him being a postman. His profession in the 1841 census was listed as a tailor in Sittingbourne High Street with his children; his wife was dead by this time. Whether he was officially employed by the post office or by the post house it is hard to say.

The post office was part of the *George,* a former post house according to *Kelly's Directory* of 1874 and it lists a William Dulake as a stationer, photographic artist and post office, trading at no. 35 High Street. Numbers 31 to 39 were part of

the original *George Hotel,* so if no. 35 was the post office, it corresponds to *Pigot's Directory* of 1862, which states 'William Thomas Dulake, *George Inn,* High St.' Could it be that the postmaster was also the innkeeper?

The landlord of the *George* in 1774 was known to have had 40 pairs of horses and W. Finch's *Historical Research of Kent,* 1803, states, 'Lishman, *George Inn,* watches – Sittingbourne Stage sets out daily from thence to Canterbury and returns same day.' Coaches had various names but mail coaches were numbered. Only the guard was employed by the post office; he wore a uniform and was armed with two pistols and a blunderbuss. He sounded a horn to warn road users to keep out of the way, as they only stopped at main post towns where the guard would toss out the mail bags to the receivers or postmasters, and snatch mail collected.

Pigot's Directory of 1826-7 lists a William Marsh as postmaster in Sittingbourne and his trade as draper. In the 1832-4 edition William Marsh is shown as being a postmaster and tailor, so it seems that not only was he a postman and a tailor but postmaster as well, or at least up to 1874 when *Kelly's Directory* only lists postmasters.

Where houses and streets had lighting, it would have been by gas and, whereas Milton's supply was publicly owned, having been set up by the commissioners in 1846, Sittingbourne's was privately owned by George Smeed. His gasworks were in Crown Quay Lane. Electricity came later, following a public notice issued in 1900 that stated the County of Kent Electrical Power Distribution Co. Ltd had the right 'to construct works, lay down wires and other apparatus and to break up streets in Sittingbourne and Milton'. Milton Council applied for electricity to be supplied in 1926 but by that time Sittingbourne and Milton were the only towns in the area not to have it. The cables were laid by 1929 but in 1934 Sittingbourne and Milton UDC voted in favour of gas for street lighting rather than electricity. A new gas holder was built in Milton in 1929. In the following year a new gas showroom and offices were built and two years after that a new, modern gas works was opened in the appropriately named Gas Road.

A much-used amenity of most towns is its library. Sittingbourne's stands in Central Avenue, but what of its past? In the closing decades of the 19th century there was the Sittingbourne Free Library that had both a lending and reference section. In 1887 the books of the Sittingbourne and Milton Book Society were offered to the town as a free public library. These books were estimated by Sotheby's as being a valuable collection. The town's ratepayers met in 1888, following the passing of the Public Libraries Act that they decided to adopt and make changes to the public room in Crescent Street so that 4,000 books could be kept there; a further 700 volumes were added in 1897.

As well as the public library, there were once other smaller privately run libraries like that of Thomas Ash and Sons, a High Street stationer, and the Chain Library on the corner of Does Alley, who lent books for 2d. per book per week.

The public library extended its opening hours in 1930 from 3 to 5p.m. and from 6 to 8p.m., except on Wednesdays, which was early closing day in the town. It joined the county council library scheme in 1931 and invested £2,000 in new books. Milton library was built in 1934 following the demolition of the old town hall and opened in 1939. Ten years later Sittingbourne library moved from Crescent Street to rooms above Burton's outfitters in the High Street and to a purpose-built building in Central Avenue in 1958.

Although the railway continued to be important to Sittingbourne during the first half of the 20th century, it was bus services that dominated public transport in the 1930s. In 1931 a new bus company, the Venture Motor Bus Co., set up in competition to the long-established Maidstone and District Motor Services Ltd. Venture's application for a licence was rejected when the Maidstone and District firm objected to it. Venture was a more popular service, being much cheaper than

78 *The cattle market.*

the Maidstone and District company, who were losing business. Venture appealed and was supported by the local council and the

town's MP but still it was rejected. The Road Traffic Commission was criticised for refusing to grant new licences but the Maidstone and District continued to dominate the local bus services. A row broke out between the bus company and the council in 1935 when they were accused of congesting the High Street. There were no bus shelters or waiting accommodation in the High Street, so the council proposed that the bus company build a bus station at the rear of their offices in East Street. This they did and the depot remained in use until well into the latter half of the 20th century. After standing empty and derelict for a number of years it was eventually demolished.

79 *The former Sittingbourne and County Bank.*

Chapter 6
Religion and Education

Religion

For most of its life Sittingbourne had only one church, St Michael's, in the High Street near where it is conjectured the original hamlet once stood. It was essentially a manorial church created to serve the parish's three principal manors, Goodneston, Bayford and Chilton. Fulston was never a manor in the true sense of the word, having been created for social reasons from a medieval estate. Although referred to as a manor, it was simply the product of early social snobbery. Such was the town's obscurity, being a part of Milton, when Archbishop Lanfranc set up the rural deaneries in the 11th century, that there was no mention of Sittingbourne in its records.

St Michael's Church is typically Norman in its method and style of construction but probably replaced an earlier wooden Saxon structure of which there is no remaining evidence, written or otherwise. It stands off-centre in its surrounding churchyard, looking almost as if, when Watling Street got to Sittingbourne, it ploughed straight through the churchyard, rather than deviate around it. St Michael's Church was appropriated to the Benedictine nunnery of Clerkenwell and remained part of its revenue until the Dissolution of the Monasteries, when it became Crown property. Elizabeth I granted it to Archbishop Parker and it became part of the archbishopric. The original 11th-century church consisted only of a nave and a chancel, which was doubled in length in the 13th century, while side aisles and the Lady Chapel were added in the 14th. The

tower, started in the 13th century, was not completed until the 15th century when the cross-aisle was extended and a rood loft was constructed. The church's five bells were recast in the 17th century to make six bells. In July 1762 the church was badly damaged by a fire that had started on its roof over the south aisle. A plumber by the name of Sherwin was attending to the lead-work and left a fire unattended while he and other workmen went off to lunch. Within an hour the whole of the roof was destroyed and the main body of the church gutted. The fire was devastating; the roof was lost, the huge timber beams that added structural integrity to the building were also destroyed and parts of the walls were unstable. Falling masonry and timbers crashing to the ground destroyed many of the tombstones and memorials both internally and externally. Many of these were later used to repair the road in front of the church. Later research has shown that the damage was so severe that the building was left in a ruinous state for a number of years afterwards; some say for as long as 20 years. The main problem was, who would pay for the repairs? By this time the manors for which the church had originally been built were no longer the powerful force they once were and could not, or would not, pay for the rebuilding work. It was left to the townspeople to raise the necessary money. Architect George Dance reported that the church could be rebuilt at a reasonable cost and so began a period of reconstruction. Improvements were made in the 1860s when a memorial stained-glass window was installed above a reredos. The seats were first fitted and the cross-aisle restored but, in the following year, attempts to restore the roof of the nave almost caused the whole building to collapse. It was then discovered that the tower seemingly had no foundations. The number of bells was increased to eight in the late 19th century and to celebrate, in 1923, a peal of 5,056 changes was rung.

The graveyard contains some fascinating tombstones, mostly of the 18th and early 19th centuries, and one of the most intriguing must surely be that of Jean Baptiste Louis Philippe, Comte de Cicquer of Normandy, a Chef d'ecadre or Admiral in the service of the king of France. The inscription is written in French and the grave lies by the western boundary path near the Iceland store. Unsuccessful efforts have been made to try to discover exactly who this admiral was; two theories have been suggested. He might have died on one of the prison hulks moored in the Medway but, if he did, why bring him here for burial? On the other hand, he might simply have died while passing through the town. The date on the headstone is believed to be 1797, which fits rather nicely with him being a refugee from the French Revolution. But there's another mystery attached to this headstone. On the reverse side is an inscription in English dedicated to an entirely different person. Could this be an early example of recycling? [See Note 2]

St Michael's served the town well until the early 19th century when Parliament voted £1m to the building of new churches under an Act of 1818. It was a period known as the era of Victorian church building, even though it commenced 17 years before her accession to the throne and concluded abruptly on her death and a change of national mood in 1901. Not since Norman times had there been such a frenzy of building new churches. It was

timely, as many of the country's churches were in ruins, having been neglected for centuries. Religious reform was not the only motive behind this Act, however. There was also a political factor designed to combat a growing continental Socialism. In part, the Act was seen by some as a thanksgiving offering for the country's deliverance from Napoleon Bonaparte and continental rationalism; it was the perfect antidote to flourishing dissent. Commissioners were appointed under the 1818 Act to sponsor the building of stately churches in the centre of many of Kent's developing towns. As a group, these churches were generally most distinctive, being Gothic in style with standard square west towers and pinnacles, and it was stipulated that all pews should be within sight of the pulpit.

This then was the heyday of Non-conformist church-building in Sittingbourne. Previously Non-conformists had met in all manner of small improvised venues; there is evidence that they met in Sittingbourne and Milton throughout the 18th century. Of these, the oldest and certainly the most widespread, in terms of having chapels in the local villages as well as the urban area, are the Methodists.

The first of this new breed of churches to be built in Sittingbourne was the Congregational Latimer Church in the High Street on the corner of Central Avenue in 1841. Before this church was built, Congregationalists had gathered at the Latimer Chapel in the Butts. After moving into the new church, the Latimer Chapel became the Sunday School until 1878 when a new Sunday School room was built in Crescent Street. After the First World War the church opened a War Memorial Institute for young people in Berry Street at the rear of the Crescent Street School Rooms. Talks began in the

80 *St Michael's Church tower, c.1916.*

81　*Interior of St Michael's Church.*

1840s about uniting the Sittingbourne and Milton Congregational churches but the two parties could not agree upon a common place of worship – was this another example of Milton's stubbornness? Eventually, in the 1970s, it was decided to close down the Milton church and the two congregations finally united. The church became known as the United Reformed Church.

This was followed in 1863 by the Wesleyan Church. John Wesley preached in Sittingbourne in 1768, 1771 and 1784 in a house that once stood in front of the original Wesleyan Methodist Church. This house was demolished in 1863 when the new church was built. The new church was quite a commanding-looking building,

built by L. Shrubsole of Faversham to a design by J. Wilson of Bath. Basically its design was in the Italian Gothic style, with a square tower topped with a spire at the front and four pointed gables. It accommodated 700 people but what made this church so unusual was that its pulpit was large enough for four people. Completing its opulence, the floor was covered with a Brussels carpet with a fleur-de-lis design and blue and crimson glass in each of the five side windows; it had state-of-the-art gas lighting and central heating. The church was enlarged in 1875 with an orchestra pit and a vestry for the minister, and the foundation stones for a new building adjoining the church were laid in 1899. It was the largest place of

82 *The former Latimer Chapel and public baths in the Butts where today St Michael's Road sweeps through.*

83 *After being deconsecrated, Milton Congregational Church was taken on as a Scouting centre but, following a severe fire, it had to be demolished. Today housing occupies the site. [Fred Littlewood]*

worship for Methodists in the urban area but Wesleyan Methodists were not the only ones to worship here.

The early building of 1863 was destroyed by incendiary bombs in February 1944 and a new church was built on the site in 1952. The foundation stone laid in October 1951 was a part of the original building.

As well as the Non-conformists, the Anglicans also needed a new church. The town's population had grown rapidly in the period of industrialisation, as had the general area of the town, so in 1867 building work began on Holy Trinity Church in Dover Street. For some years previously, Anglicans living in this part of the town had congregated in a room in Pembury Street until they could raise enough money to build a proper church. By 1865 £1,300 of the estimated £3,600 needed for the new church had been raised and the work began. Designed by R.C. Hussey, it was officially opened for worship on 2 October 1886, although much of the work was still incomplete. It later caused a Mr T. Lake of Tonge to write to the local newspaper, commenting that:

> … having seen three large buildings erected in Sittingbourne as Dissenting places of worship, while the half-finished structure at the top of the town represented the effort of the churchmen of this district to provide for the spiritual wants of the rapidly increased population in the locality in which it is erected.

A public appeal was launched and, by 1873, the building work was finally completed, the original building having been extended by some 23ft and side aisles added. The harmonium was replaced by an organ in 1879 and a reredos erected beneath the east window. A plan to replace

the single bell with a peal of six was mooted in 1895 but it was found that major works to the tower would be necessary to take the extra weight, so the plan was scrapped. The vestry was added in 1898 and the Lady Chapel in 1902.

Meanwhile the room in Pembury Street became a school room and a church hall where social and fund-raising events could be held. The new church was formally assigned a district by Queen Victoria in 1869, which meant that wedding ceremonies could be conducted there. The church played a major social and religious role in the community and in 1906 a much larger hall was opened alongside the church. Holy Trinity was innovative in leading the way in the use of lay people to undertake readings, setting up a children's corner and holding a Good Friday Procession of Witness. It was suggested that the church be united with St Mary's in Park Road in the 1970s but, after much discussion, St Mary's united with St Michael's; Holy Trinity then became linked to Bobbing church.

What made this church different from all the rest of those built at this time is that it is built of Kentish ragstone to a traditional church design rather than brick in a Gothic design, which gave Holy Trinity the appearance of having been on site for much longer than it really had.

The next Non-conformist church to be built here was the Baptist Tabernacle in West Street. In April 1866 the Rev. Spurgeon, a leading English Baptist minister, preached at St Michael's Church in aid of funds for building a Baptist Tabernacle here. Later that same year the Baptist Sunday School was started and the West Street site purchased. The Rev. Spurgeon returned to Sittingbourne the following year to lay the foundation stone and the tabernacle was opened for worship

84   *Holy Trinity Church, Dover Street, 1907.*

85   *Holy Trinity Church, Dover Street in 2007 looking remarkably unchanged after 140 years. [Barry Kinnersley]*

86 *East Street featuring the United Methodist Church on the right, 1971. [Fred Atkins]*

in October 1867. It cost £1,700 to build and was designed by local architect, W.L. Grant. It was a plain brick structure built by Luke Phillips, Junior of Milton Regis, with a seating capacity for 500; provision was made for a gallery to be added later. It was installed in 1886, giving the tabernacle much-needed extra seating. The Rev. Doubleday was appointed minister in 1881, a post he held for 40 years.

This was a time of rapid expansion in the Baptist faith and in 1884 a Sunday School building was added to the west side of the church with a memorial hall and other rooms following in January 1897. Such was the following by the Baptists the Sunday School building had to be enlarged by 1901 and mission rooms were later opened in Flushing Street, Milton

Regis and Bayford Road, Sittingbourne.

In 1881 a group of Methodists known as the Primitive Methodists announced a plan to build a chapel in Shakespeare Road, Sittingbourne. It opened for worship in 1869 but by 1871 was far too small, so a new building was planned, keeping the old chapel as a schoolroom. The new chapel, built in front of the old one, opened in 1883 and was designed by Sittingbourne architect W.L. Grant; the builder was High and Monk. It had seating for 250 people. Primitive Methodism was also strong in Milton Regis.

In 1859 the Bible Christian Society opened a chapel at St George's Street, Snipeshill and in 1879 there were plans for them to have a new chapel in East Street but the foundation stone was not laid until

87   *By 1999 the church had become a martial arts centre. [Barry Kinnersley]*

October 1887; it was another design by architect W.L. Grant. The Bible Christian Society became the United Methodist Church in the 20th century but the church was closed and sold in 1980 upon amalgamation with the former Wesleyan church and is now a martial arts centre.

The last of Sittingbourne's late 19th-century churches to be built was the Roman Catholic Church of the Sacred Heart in West Street in 1892, following a revival in the Catholic religion. Prior to this, mass had been celebrated in various private houses throughout the town. In March 1892 there had been a number of anti-Catholic talks held in the town hall but, despite this, later in the same year a chapel, school and a house for the priest were built in West Street; the first public

mass was held on 20 November that same year. The following year an open-air service was held with the Litany being read in Latin and in 1894 the convent school was built in a previously private residence, Schamel, the home of solicitor Mr Gibson on the corner of Ufton Lane, as a convent and boarding school for young ladies.

The move towards getting a Roman Catholic church built here was started by Bishop John Butt who, in 1892, had found a suitable site to the west of the town, an area known as the Rock estate. There he established a mission consisting of a school, a chapel and a presbytery and appointed Father Eugene O'Sullivan to run it. He was a young and ambitious Irish priest who stayed in Sittingbourne for 15 years. To some

88 *To help raise money to build the Roman Catholic church, small boys were sent out to sell bricks for 1s. per hod. [Courtesy of the* East Kent Gazette*]*

89   *West Street facing east, featuring the Catholic church.*

90 *West Street facing west.*

it might have seemed like a daunting prospect to raise £5,000 for a church for a minority faith in a relatively poor town, but those who doubted had not taken into consideration the enthusiasm and fighting spirit of Father O'Sullivan. He appealed for money in some of the leading Catholic magazines and received donations from as far away as China, Russia and Persia. Typical of his appeals is the verse he wrote that said:

> For anyone who hasn't yet sent
> a brick or tile for the church in Kent
> the penitent season of Lent
> is a most suitable season in which to repent.

He also used children, sending them out onto the streets with sign boards asking for 1s. a hod for bricks. It was a form of fund-raising that was not liked by Sittingbourne's residents and Father O'Sullivan encountered a lot of hostile reaction.

The new church was designed by local architect W.L. Grant and its foundation stone was laid in 1901; it was consecrated and opened for worship in 1902. The 'Angelus Chime' of eight bells rang out in 1905 and in 1910 the first Requiem mass to take place in Sittingbourne since the Reformation was performed. During the 1930s the church bought the West Street Assembly Hall from the Liberal Party, renaming it the Whitefriars Hall, the Carmelite Order returned from exile and took over the running of the church, and the Carmel Hall in Ufton Lane was opened for social events. The Roman Catholics were now a part of the town's religious life. The Roman Catholic school built in 1896 had accommodation for 141 pupils but only 30 to 40 pupils attended it.

Although strictly within the parish of Milton Regis, St Mary's in Park Road has long been regarded as one of Sittingbourne's churches, built in response to an increasing population in this part of the parish. Of all the Anglican churches that lay within a one-and-a-half-mile radius of the town centre, St Mary's is the youngest and probably the least attractive externally. A casual traveller going up Park Road could pass by without even noticing it and, of all our local churches, St Mary's must be the one most people know least about. It has neither a churchyard nor a surrounding open space and is squeezed between the neighbouring houses. Even the entrance to the church is hard to find but it has a magnificent interior with a lofty nave. Although St Mary's cannot be described as being an architectural masterpiece, it comes close to being what many would describe as their ideal church, constructed of red brick and offering a warm and homely atmosphere.

When the Rev. T.T. Lucius Morgan was appointed vicar of Holy Trinity Church, Milton in the early 1900s he quickly realised how vast his new parish was. It extended from the Swale in the north to the top of Gore Court Road in the south. He called a meeting of a number of influential parishioners, started a building fund and purchased a site in Park Road upon which to build a church for his congregation living south of the main road, the A2. The Rev. Morgan launched an appeal around the Deanery and the largest donation of £100 was received from Edward Lloyd. The diocese promised a further £2,000 for the proposed church and work began in 1901 when Archbishop Frederick Temple laid the foundation stone; it was consecrated by the Bishop of Dover, the Rt. Rev. W. Walsh, and opened for worship in January 1902. The architect was Mr R. Philip Day. It was originally planned to have a south aisle and a tower at the western end but as the estimate for this exceeded the available funds it was decided to build only the chancel and nave. It was discovered during building works that, unless a vestry and lady chapel were built there would have to be substantial flying buttresses to prevent the high chancel arch from collapsing, so a loan from Martin's Bank was obtained for the work.

The first curate-in-charge was the Rev. S.B. Ritso, an energetic and likeable priest who remained in post until 1908, after which the Rev. R. de B. Saunderson succeeded him. He had previously been the curate at Holy Trinity Church, Dover Street and lived in a house that later became the Cedars Club in the High Street next to the Baptist Tabernacle. St Mary's flourished under him until his death in 1912.

Following the First World War, when Kemsley paper mill and village were built, it became increasingly difficult for a vicar and a curate to cover this vast parish so, following the appointment of a new vicar of Milton in 1924, it was decided to make the St Mary's district a separate parish. The new parish was formalised in 1925 with its own vicar, the Rev. H.J. King from Croydon, who initially lived in a small house at the top of Park Road but he made it his priority to find a suitable site for a permanent vicarage. He purchased a piece of land in Albany Road, opposite the recreation ground, from Mr A. Reynolds for £400 and building work began straight away; the Rev. and Mrs King moved in 1927. The building costs were borne by the diocese. The Rev. King served the parish

91 *St Mary's Church, Park Road. [Barry Kinnersley]*

well until his retirement in 1935 when a collection amounting to £18 10s. 0d. was presented to him.

By the time the next vicar, the Rev. T.H. Jacques, was appointed it was becoming clear that the parish hall in Ufton Lane was seriously in need of attention. It was decided to sell the site and with the money build the present hall and boiler room at the end of the church. The new hall was designed by Mr Reg Kift, built by local builders Wraight Ltd and officially opened by the Bishop of Dover, the Rt. Rev. Rose, in 1937. Iron railings and a gate were added to the front of the church in Park Road and a gate behind it in Unity Street, a gift of the Bloxland family, but the fencing was later taken away to help the war effort.

At the outbreak of war the Rev. Jacques volunteered to become an army chaplain in the Brigade of Guards and the day-to-day running of the parish was put in the hands of a curate-in-charge, the Rev. Alan Webb. In 1944, while still serving in the army, the Rev. Jacques resigned, the Rev. Webb left the parish and a familiar figure to many of Sittingbourne's older residents, the Rev. W. McN. Bradshaw, came to the parish. He quickly made a dynamic impact by joining the Civil Defence Corps as an Air Raid Warden and starting the parish's

Cub and Scout troops. Soon after settling in he married and his wife started the Girl Guide Company. A Belgian oak choir screen, part of the original fixtures and fittings, was removed and exchanged for two pine choir stalls from Milton church but unfortunately Milton church was not allowed to use the screen as it wanted to and it eventually went to a church in Shoreham, Sussex. As it was being used so extensively, the hall needed toilet facilities so a fund was started, selling bricks at 1s. each; Christmas carols were sung around the parish, and the toilets were built at a cost of £400. The church celebrated its Golden Jubilee in 1952 with a sermon preached by the Archbishop of Canterbury, Dr Geoffrey Fisher, and its Diamond Jubilee in 1962, this time addressed by the newly appointed Archbishop of Canterbury, Dr Michael Ramsey.

With so many churches so close together, in an age of declining congregations, it gave rise to discussion about the need for so many churches. There was much talk about closures and amalgamations and it is to the credit of the parishioners of St Mary's that they faced the closure of their church steadfastly. But this was later seen to be the wrong answer and, instead, a group of clergy was given the task of finding a pattern of ministry suitable for the town. This was when it was decided to amalgamate St Mary's with St Michael's to form a joint benefice.

Education

Before the 19th century education had been of little importance, being the preserve of the more well-to-do, and lay in the hands of the Church authorities. The first Elementary Education Bill was put before Parliament in 1870 and the situation here was much the same as elsewhere in the country. There was a choice between the Church-controlled national schools and a number of private schools of variable standards. Our oldest school at this time was St Michael's National School, which had started in 1812 to teach both boys and girls aged six to 14 the basic 'three Rs' and the principles of the Christian religion. The school was funded by annual subscriptions from pupils, an annual collection taken in the church and weekly 'pence money' for each child attending. Until 1840 the school was held in a boarded-off section of the church but in 1846 a new school was built in the Butts, an area now covered by St Michael's Road; it accommodated 160 pupils. It was in the same area as the infants' school, which had been built in 1839 and funded by the Vallance family, who also had local interests in banking and a brewery. The Canterbury Diocesan Board of Education awarded a grant of £60 towards the cost of enlarging this school in 1866.

The Elementary Act sought to complete the voluntary system by retaining efficient schools and plugging gaps to provide an education for all children aged five to thirteen. Districts were given a year in which to provide sufficient school places through voluntary schemes; otherwise School Boards would be set up and schools provided, using money collected by increasing the rates. Members of the Church of England, led by the Bishop of Dover, met in October 1870 to discuss whether the 300 places needed in Sittingbourne should be met by extending and increasing the number of the town's national schools, or opt for a rate-aided school. The majority voted in favour of continuing the national schools system whereby they were ensured continued religious teaching. It was said, 'The moral effects of these schools were obvious to all.' As a result of this meeting, a committee was set up and a subscription started to raise money for a new national school.

The thought of secular education being funded by increased rates was an anathema to the Non-conformists who opposed the proposal; the Methodists met and decided to enlarge their Sunday School room to accommodate their own day school. The foundation stone was laid in May 1873 and the Wesleyan day school opened in January 1874; it accommodated 150 pupils. Earlier, in May 1872, Holy Trinity National School opened in Spring Street next door to the church; it cost £900 and accommodated 300 children. The opening of this school led to the closure of the infants' school in the Butts in March 1873.

Despite the town's best efforts to provide new schools, by 1877, with a steadily increasing population and new bylaws demanding compulsory attendance at an efficient school for all children from five to 13, there were many problems. A report highlighted the fact that, of the 1,624 children of school age, only 881 were attending public elementary schools and 76 at 'efficient private schools'; 164 children were attending 'inefficient private schools' while 503 were not attending school at all. It was pointed out many children were refused admission to some of the schools because they had no shoes or stockings, or they did not know the basic alphabet. This was in violation of the Education Act and the guilty parties faced losing their funding. The problem of 'unacceptable children' was most acute in Milton Regis. In their defence, the school's proprietors said that accepting these children lowered the school's standards and consequently their income. The grant they received depended on how well the children did in the annual public examinations.

The Education Department issued an ultimatum in 1879 to the effect that, if places were not found for over 350 children, a School Board would be set up to take control of education in Sittingbourne. The national system of elementary education was still in place locally in 1894 and, as no fees were being charged, it was not necessary to set up the School Board. Over the following years more and more schools were built in both Sittingbourne and Milton Regis to accommodate the population explosion and the private schools continued to flourish.

Education was now being offered to adults as well as children. From as early as the 1850s evening classes were run at private residences throughout the town. In 1866 St Michael's Night School was awarded a grant of £2 10s. 0d. to further its work. Very soon recognised examinations, like the Examinations of the Science and Art Department of South Kensington, were being held. Classes had also been held in the town hall but in 1904 they were moved to a room at Brenchley House. By 1919 an adult education school for men had opened at the Butts and in 1938 a wooden building was erected in the grounds of Brenchley House, known as the technical institute. It doubled as an annexe to the school during the day. This building was later moved to Central Avenue where to this day it serves the community as a meeting place for local organisations and societies, and is known as the Phoenix Centre or Phoenix House; it is known by different names to different people. When in 1973 Brenchley House was no longer being used as a school, the adult education centre moved into the main building until 1978 when it moved to College Road.

Radical changes in the education system came in 1902 with a second major Education Act. It meant that ratepayers now had to pay for education and those voluntary schools that did not reach exacting new standards would be replaced by new council schools. This angered the Non-conformists who set up the Sittingbourne and Milton Passive Resistance Committee. They argued that the Act violated conscience by making them pay for instruction that was unscriptural, ignored citizens' rights by taxing them without representation, was detrimental to the interests of education and there was no moral sanction for it as education had not been an issue upon which the government had been elected. The campaigners refused to pay the full council rate by deducting the education element from it. They were prosecuted in October 1903 and, after leaving the police court, they joined an open-air protest meeting outside the Baptist Tabernacle. An auction was later held to raise money to pay their fines.

One of the first benefits of the new Act was the opening in October 1904 of the County School, later known as the girls' grammar school, at Brenchley House.

Initially, it held 28 full-time pupils and 48 older pupil-teachers who received part-time education. The new school became officially recognised by the Board of Education in 1905. In the following year the school amalgamated with the Sittingbourne High School for Girls, a former private school that, since the 1890s, had occupied the adjoining premises. Meanwhile Borden Grammar School for boys, another former privately run school, established itself as a day school after its headmaster left, taking most of the boarders with him. The girls' grammar school occupied Brenchley House until 1958 when it moved to a new purpose-built school in Highsted Road. Brenchley House was then home to Sittingbourne East Girls' School until 1969 when they too moved to a new purpose-built school known as Rowena Girls' School, in Swanstree Avenue. The East Girls' School consisted of two classes of 11-year-olds from the West Secondary School from where, due to overcrowding, they had to move out with two teachers.

92 *The County School, Brenchley House, c.1916.*

93 *Brenchley House, 1998, no longer a school but a collection of offices housing a number of different businesses. [Barry Kinnersley]*

94   *The original Borden Grammar School in College Road. [Picture by Barry Kinnersley]*

This was the last of the four new secondary schools to be built in the town following the Education Act of 1944, which raised the school leaving age to sixteen. The other two new secondary schools were Sittingbourne West Secondary School, now known as Westlands, and St John's, now known as Sittingbourne Community College.

The Kent County Council's Education Committee conducted a review of elementary education in the county in 1905, which showed that there were 10 schools in Sittingbourne and Milton Regis but, as the Pembury Street Infants' School and the Wesleyan school did not have satisfactory premises, it chose not to recognise them. This led to the building

of the town's first council school at Gaze Hill in 1909. Mr Roper, who had been headmaster of the Wesleyan school since it opened in 1874, became headmaster of the new school and remained there until he retired in 1919 after more than 50 years as a teacher. The cost of repairs to the Pembury Street Infants' School proved to be too costly so in March 1920 the school closed.

The Sittingbourne and District Education Board, which was responsible for elementary schools, maintaining secondary schools and further education, was set up in the early 1920s. By the end of that decade Borden Grammar School had moved from its College Road building to new premises in the Avenue of Remembrance and their former premises

95   *The 'new' Borden Grammar School in the Avenue of Remembrance. [Barry Kinnersley]*

became the Kent Farm Institute in 1930. After the KFI moved out in the mid-1960s the building was used firstly as a teacher training college, the first in Kent for mature students, and in 1978 it became the adult education centre.

The location of the new secondary and primary schools reflects the growth of post-war housing in the town. From the 1950s onwards the old schools were becoming overcrowded and insufficient in number to meet the increasing population's needs, so several new primary schools were built to meet this need. The first such school was in Barrow Grove on the Homewood Avenue Estate. As other housing estates were built, so too were new schools to meet the need. Pre-1903 schools that still served their purpose were given a facelift.

Chapter 7

Twentieth-Century Civic Development

Sittingbourne today is very different from how it was 150 years or so ago. It is not a town people visit for the quality of its shops or sightseeing and has never made the most of its history or heritage. Most of the early buildings in the High Street, except for the inns, would have been private houses from where, in some cases, businesses would have been conducted; shops in the form we know today did not exist. The town seized every opportunity to improve and expand, helped to a large degree by the coming of the railway in 1858 when London became more easily accessible. The town's economy radically changed from an agrarian-based dependency to industrialisation and the growth of these industries led in turn to a significant rise in Sittingbourne's population from 3,000 in 1801, to 8,000 by 1861 and 16,800 by 1921.

After the electrification of the railway in the 1950s the town started to attract London-bound commuters and new housing estates were needed to accommodate this new sector of our population. These new estates gradually eroded the town's remaining surrounding agricultural land, a practice that is still continuing as we enter the 21st century. The town's population had risen to 23,600 in 1961 and by 2001 it had increased to 41,409 but, with further expansion of the town very much to the fore, this figure will significantly increase in the not too distant future.

Before the construction of St Michael's Road, all traffic had to pass through the High Street but by the 1930s the situation had become so bad, especially on bank holidays, that a traffic census was held; up to 960 vehicles an hour were passing through. One solution to this problem came from an unlikely source. In 1945 the council acquired a 58-acre site in Canterbury Road upon which to build the second of their new large housing estates. A narrow peripheral strip of this site could be used for part of the much-needed ring road, so Swanstree Avenue was built on its eastern side to form the start of this road. Plans showed that it would partly circumnavigate the estate before cutting through an agricultural belt of land and returning to the urban area of the Ufton Lane Estate, now Homewood Avenue, then on to Borden Lane, into what is now Adelaide Drive and back on to the A2 road. Despite the county council's careful planning of the road and the local council accepting it with certain modifications, the plan was subsequently abandoned. There are still tangible reminders of this ring road to be seen to this day. It is not quite so obvious in Swanstree Avenue but elsewhere, like Brenchley Road, Capel Road and Homewood Avenue, there are wide sections of carriageway that look strangely out of place.

Another survey conducted in 1950 showed that the traffic flow figure had dramatically increased to 1,500 and by 1954 it had increased even further, to over 5,000 vehicles an hour. The government responded by building the M2 motorway to the south of the town in the early 1960s. The motorway greatly alleviated the problem but there was still an urgent need to remove

96 *One of the last steam trains to pull out of Sittingbourne. [Chris Deamer]*

97   *The start of the proposed Sittingbourne ring road at Swanstree Avenue. [Mick Clancy]*

through-traffic from the High Street. In the early 1970s a ring road running north of the High Street from West Street to Canterbury Road, cutting through some of the town's

derelict and slum areas, was built. The High Street was then pedestrianised on Saturdays only, in 1980.

One area of the town that has undergone a remarkable change in the last 50 years is Central Avenue, linking the High Street to the Avenue of Remembrance. It is a road of some note, representing one man's dream of a much-needed centrally placed civic centre. By the early part of the 20th century Sittingbourne had grown considerably in size, having amalgamated with Milton Regis and Murston. Its range of responsibilities and duties had grown enormously but, despite this, the individual council departments had never been housed together in one civic centre. Sittingbourne's Town Hall, built as a corn exchange in 1859, stood on the corner of Central Avenue and the High Street, a site now occupied by the NatWest Bank,

98   *A further section of the proposed ring road at Homewood Avenue. [Mick Clancy]*

but it was never used to house the various council departments. The town clerk's and treasurer's departments, for example, were in offices above Burton's the outfitters; the surveyor's department was at Lydbrook House opposite the *Coniston Hotel* in London Road; the public health officer was at Johnson House in Burley Road and the housing department was located in a High Street shop. It was an unsatisfactory arrangement.

A new town clerk, Don Allen, was appointed in 1948 and he felt the time was right to review the town's future development. A meeting of representatives of the various public service bodies and council departments was convened to discuss the development of a civic centre for the town, and borough engineer and surveyor Maurice Lashmar drew up an imaginative plan for the centre, which was

to be built on undeveloped land between the High Street and the Avenue of Remembrance. Consideration was given to public services like the police, fire brigade, the county education department, the bus company, the inland revenue and the post office into the one central area. If space permitted, Mr Lashmar further envisaged a recreational area with a replacement for the town's dilapidated swimming baths. The plan generated considerable interest but, due to restricted access and deployment, the bus company, whose depot at that time was in East Street, and the fire brigade, in the High Street next to the Baptist church, declined the invitation to move.

The first buildings in this new road were erected in 1961 and were designated for the inland revenue and the post office; there was already a new telephone exchange

99 *The Avenue of Remembrance where every tree is dedicated to local men who died in the First World War.*

on site serving over 2,200 subscribers, 850 more than at the old site in the High Street where Argos now is. The library, which had since 1948 been located above Montague Burton's in the High Street, relocated in 1953, to a temporary building situated behind the town hall while a new library was being built and was opened by author H.E. Bates in 1958; it was further extended in 1971. Sittingbourne's library service is much older than most people realise. It began as a free public library in premises in Crescent Street, where the entrance to the Forum now is, in 1888 owned by Mrs Hester George. She and her husband Frederick lived above the library. Mrs George operated the library on her own until 1921 when she was 80 years old. The council appointed a part-time assistant to help her and Mrs George finally retired at the age of 90 in 1931.

Next it was decided to bring all the various council departments into one central building to be erected on the corner of Central Avenue and the Avenue of Remembrance. The work was finished in 1965 ahead of schedule but the new civic centre was short-lived as in 1974, following major local government reform, Sittingbourne and Milton Urban District Council amalgamated with Sheppey, Faversham and Swale Rural District Councils to form the unified district of Swale. As a new and much larger authority it needed larger premises and a suitable office block standing empty on the corner of the High Street and East Street was ideal. It had been designed and built to attract companies from London into the town but had stood empty for a number of years. After the 1974 Act the new council bought the building, moved in and named it Swale House.

The police authority meanwhile had begun their own building programme to replace the outdated police station on the corner of Park Road and West Street, which later became the magistrates' court, with a new station in Central Avenue. By the late 1990s it also had become too small for modern requirements so they took over the former income tax office next door, as it had been left empty some years earlier, to supplement the existing police station.

The new, much-needed ring road, St Michael's Road, was constructed in 1973. As it sliced its way through the northern part of the town, several historically important buildings like St Michael's vicarage, the Butts School and the Latimer Chapel as well as many tiny back streets and lanes were lost forever. The ambulance service moved into their new headquarters in Crown Quay Lane in 1963 though St Michael's Road was not fully opened and gave only limited access. The fire brigade had to wait until 1981 before it could relocate from the High Street to its new station in St Michael's Road. It was certainly a decade or two of major changes for Sittingbourne and, in part, a realisation of Mr Lashmar's grand plan.

The old civic centre, now with a new building standing before it, erected in 2005–6 for the town's community organisations, is used partly as the Swallows Leisure Centre with its modern swimming pool, opened by HRH Princess Anne in 1989, which replaced the old pool in the Butts. The old council chamber has been redesigned to accommodate the Avenue Theatre and an Age Concern day centre fronts onto the Avenue of Remembrance. In front of this building in Central Avenue is a clock tower. The actual clock was once housed in a cupola above the town hall but, after it was demolished in 1969, the clock was put in storage until a new use could be found for it. The Sittingbourne Society suggested that it be mounted in a brick-built tower outside the new civic centre to

100 *The old clock from the demolished town hall in its new setting, 1999. [Picture by Barry Kinnersley]*

commemorate the wedding of HRH Prince Charles and Lady Diana Spencer in 1981.

Central Avenue runs into a T-junction with the Avenue of Remembrance, a war memorial, lined with trees, at the base of each of which is a bronze plaque inscribed with the name and other details of a local serviceman killed in the First World War. It was laid out in 1923, the work being undertaken as an unemployment relief scheme. Since the original planting, many of the trees and plaques have had to be replaced but in the stretch of the avenue running from the main section up to the recreation ground, many of the originals remain intact.

Standing between the former civic centre and the library is a nondescript timber building known as the Phoenix Centre, where local societies and organisations hold meetings. It was erected in the grounds of the girls' grammar school in the High Street in 1938 and moved to its current location after the school sold its playing

101 *The old town hall sketched by David Colthup during its demolition in August 1969.*

field so that the Central Avenue plan could be accomplished. Further down Central Avenue, nearer the High Street and standing behind the United Reformed Church, is the town's war memorial, which originally stood in the recreation ground in Albany Road. It was built in 1921 and paid for by public subscription, but was moved to its present location in 1990, where it was set in a small memorial garden. It is topped by a bronze wreath, the work of local sculptor Ann Flewers, the bronze having been taken from memorial plaques that could not be resited in the Avenue of Remembrance when Sainsbury's supermarket moved there. Just around the corner, at the side of the church, is a memorial to local servicemen who have won the VC, Britain's highest military award. It was dedicated in 1995 to mark the 50th anniversary of VE Day. Without any shadow of doubt, Central Avenue gave Sittingbourne a much-needed point of focus.

While the High Street had served shoppers well for many centuries, in the 1970s it was supplemented by a shopping centre, The Forum, which was built on land behind the High Street shops. The entrance is the former Crescent Street, whose nameplate can still clearly be seen on the side walls of corner shops. Several roads were lost when this shopping centre was built, roads like Berry Street, Railway Terrace, Cross Street, *et al.* Together with St Michael's Road it totally changed the face of the area in front of the railway station.

The 1970s can best be remembered as being a time of major changes that have completely altered the face and character of Sittingbourne; never before had such extensive changes been made, but more was to come. A few years later much of the former industrial area north of the railway line on the banks of the creek that had formerly been used for brick-fields was cleared away and an industrial estate of small factories and businesses built thereon. A new road, Eurolink Way/Mill Way, swept through it, following very closely the line of the old Lower Road,

102   *The Phoenix Centre, the former adult education centre when it stood in the grounds of the girls' grammar school.*

connecting Milton Regis to Murston. This new estate also took in much of the former slum area of Milton Regis where rubble from the demolished buildings was used to fill in parts of the creek. Anyone who moved away from the town 50 or 60 years ago would hardly recognise certain areas now.

In looking towards the future further changes are envisaged that will again alter the town's character. The council has a rolling local plan, a document drawn up partly in response to government demands, which looks at future development, planning, shopping and living requirements in the town. It has far-reaching implications but its implementation is far

103 *The Co-op in East Street, c.1920.*

into the future, the subject perhaps of a future book on the town's history.

104 *When the High Street was refurbished and pedestrianised in 1996 it was decided to create a focal point by erecting a statue of a bargeman and his dog to commemorate the town's former barge industry. The statue is the work of Jill Tweed, FRSB and it was unveiled by the Mayor of Swale, Cllr E. Madgwick, in June 1996.*

Appendix

Town Life 50 Years Ago

For many centuries much of Sittingbourne and its surrounding area remained unchanged as a small market town despite all the industrial developments that were taking place. A massive house-building programme had taken place between 1840 and 1910 to house the town's growing population. If you stepped back 50 years to say, 1956, you'd hardly notice any differences in the town at all; fashions have not significantly changed and the traffic passing through the High Street would not be that different from today's. Goods available in the shops would certainly be familiar. But, in going back a hundred years to 1906, we would most certainly see some marked differences. In the second half of the 20th century the pace of outward change appears to have slowed down, perhaps due in part to advances in technological achievements that have affected all of our lives, but house building continued apace. In comparison, the first half of the 20th century saw dramatic changes brought about by two wars on a global scale, a catalyst that in turn created major changes in society.

In the records of the town's heritage museum there is an excellent snapshot of life in the town in the 1950s. The secretary of the Sittingbourne and Milton Business Women's Club, Miss E. Venus, said in her annual report '… in just three-quarters of a century Sittingbourne has grown from a small market town to a busy industrial town whose products are world-famous'. Its population has increased significantly from 450 in the 14th century, when the town had only 90 houses, to 5,000 in 1856, a figure that included Milton as well, to 19,838 in 1930 and 21,970 in 1956. By this time the paper mills were the principal employers and unemployment was only 0.6 per cent of the population compared with a national average of 1.2 per cent. The mill introduced a Sick Benefit Scheme for its 4,500 workers in 1956 funded entirely by the employers, offering up to 25 per cent of the employees' basic wage for a maximum of 26 weeks if they became ill.

Brickmaking was slowly going into decline, although the demand for Stock bricks remained high, but competition and production costs were causing concern. The general availability of brickearth was made increasingly difficult by the Town and Country Planning Act, which had complex procedures for acquiring land for excavation and imposed stringent demands. In trying to put a brave front on a bad situation, the Associated Portland Cement Company held a family fun day for its workers and their families in West Lane Meadows. It was attended by about ten thousand people.

What were wages like 50 years ago? Between 1948 and 1954 wages rose by 52 per cent; agricultural workers, for example, earned £3 p.w., less than their factory-based colleagues and they had longer working hours. Needless to say, this caused a huge migration from the land to the factories. It was a situation further speeded up by cheap imports of fruit from Europe.

The weather in 1956 was predictable, with long, hot summers and cold winters. Or was it? Our chief concern was not about holes in the ozone layer but smog created by the extensive use of coal fires. We tend to look back on the weather conditions of the past through rose-tinted spectacles but records show that, while Easter 1956 started off chilly, by Easter Monday it had warmed up quite considerably and the Whitsun Bank Holiday was one of the finest for years. However, when the town's carnival was held on 3 July the local newspaper reported that it was bitterly cold, rained and the wind blew. Things hadn't improved by August when an 80mph gale swept through the town, causing flooding and widespread damage to roofs and TV aerials. A week later another freak storm with hailstones and flooding arrived. In looking back to the weather of yesteryear we tend to forget about such things.

A 'hung' council was elected in May 1956 consisting of nine Labour members, four Conservative members and five Independent members, but the populace were not unduly worried; the council was stretched for funds and among the casualties was the Central Avenue development plan. The council even had to decline a request made by the Royal British Legion for £5 to decorate the town's Carnival Queen float. Many fêtes and carnivals were held in the 1950s; hardly was there a weekend without one and they were popular. The Labour Party attracted over 13,000 to their monster fête, which featured the legendary Dagenham Girl Pipers and a marksman who missed the target and accidentally shot his wife who was holding it. The St John Ambulance vehicle would not start so local MP Percy Wells had to take the unfortunate lady to hospital in his car.

Fly-tipping is not a new trend. Back in 1956 the chief sanitary inspector expressed concern over the number of sites around the town where rubbish was frequently dumped. These sites included both council and privately owned land, in particular College Road. Such was the volume that he expressed his amazement at how often people appeared to be changing their beds and furniture.

It is not a bad thing to stop periodically and take stock of our progress, or lack of it, to see what lessons can be learned and from this to make improvements to the future. It remains to be seen what our successors of 2056 will make of our life in 2006.

Notes

1. After this manuscript had been submitted, Alan Abbey, chairman of the Historical Research Group of Sittingbourne, presented me with a most interesting hypothesis regarding the town's origins, which, if true, sheds a whole new light on the matter. Given the conjectured location of the original early settlement, in an area known as Bayford on the bank of Milton Creek, it's fair to assume that it stood at a ford across the creek where the Lower Road track way crossed it. A ford would be considered a major resource and its ownership highly prized for taxes and control of movement, etc., so it would have given that early settlement a purpose. I asked what the 'Bay' element of the name might refer to and was told it was a corruption of 'Babbe', probably a Saxon name as no Celtic names have survived here. However, Mr Abbey foresaw a problem with this explanation, as the ford would have been so close to Watling Street as to make the Lower Road track way little used. It must, therefore, have originated prior to the Roman invasion of A.D. 43, making Babbe a later 'owner'. The Saxon chieftain Saeda, after whom the town is said to have been named, may have set up a settlement in the vicinity but the actual ford was likely to have been controlled or owned by Babbe, a Saxon of much higher status. It has been suggested that Babbe was a very early arrival amongst the Saxons and already controlled the ford when Saeda arrived. Alternatively, Babbe might have died and his descendants controlled the ford; the name had simply stuck. We have to break down early Saxon Kent into quite

different portions from parishes to see any kind of ownership/control patterns.

Some historians consider that Babbe had his settlement at what is now Bavinge (i.e. Babbes people), near Stelling Minnis, according to Mr Abbey. Today it is a farm with a wood nearby, but at one time it would have been a centre for a reasonably important person. It is likely that he was financially responsible for the upkeep of the ford and the section of road, which may explain the distance between Bayford and Bavinge.

Mr Abbey sees the early settlement of the Bayford site as being just a small house or loose hamlet located at the ford, left nameless until later, and then by association only. It was not a big enough settlement to warrant its own name until a map of the area was drawn, whereupon it became official. Bayford did not become a manor until quite late, possibly not until Sittingbourne was created as a separate parish in about 1150.

If this hypothesis has any truth attached to it, it sheds an entirely new light on how Sittingbourne came into being, but, like the hypothesis about Saeda, without any firm evidence it can only remain just a theory. It is up to you, the reader, to decide which explanation you prefer.

2. Shortly before finalising the manuscript, further information came to light about Jean-Baptiste Louis Philippe, the Count of Cacqueray, which throws light on who he was and how he came to be buried in Sittingbourne. The de Cacqueray family wrote to the chairman of the Historical

Research Group of Sittingbourne, Alan Abbey, who, with the help of Harry Cox, head of languages at Fulston Manor School, translated the letter, which gave a fascinating insight into the life of the family's remarkable ancestor.

The de Cacqueray family can trace their ancestry back to the Middle Ages when they were involved in the manufacture of glass, bringing many new innovations to the industry. Jean-Baptiste was the third son of the Lord of Valmenier and was born in Rochefort, France on 1 May 1730. At the age of 15 he was sent to join the coastguard service and was promoted to the rank of ensign in 1751. In 1757 he was assigned to a ship in the French navy, the *Duke of Burgundy*, where he was promoted to the rank of lieutenant. His ship was sent to Canada to help defend what was then a French province. By 1763 he and his brother and brother-in-law had been reassigned to the man o' war *The Strange* and they fought in the waters beyond Brest against the British fleet under the command of Admiral Hawke. The French fleet was commanded by an old and indecisive commander who failed to control his ships and was forced to flee in the face of the superior British fleet, bad weather and dangerous reefs. But despite such disasters befalling his superiors, Jean-Baptiste was dubbed Knight of St Louis in 1763.

During a shaky period of peace Jean-Baptiste signed a marriage contract with Marie-Louise de Pradel in 1767, although he did not marry her until 1782; presumably she was still a minor when the contract was signed. By 1771 he had been promoted to captain and given command of a frigate and a year later was appointed captain of a man o' war, the 64-gun *Proteus*. The American Revolution saw hostilities between France and England begin in earnest once again and Jean-Baptiste saw action throughout, although he missed the major sea battle of

the conflict as his ship was docked in the West Indies undergoing repairs.

The next period in his life becomes confusing as the family history seems to contradict itself by giving Jean-Baptiste two quite different roles at the same time. He is listed in 1775 as being a major in the French Marine Corps and was promoted to brigadier in the Navy in 1781. In 1782, as captain of the 74-gun *Beloved* he is recorded as attacking an English convoy and chasing Admiral Howe to Gibraltar. It would seem that the two titles may go together with his office of brigadier being paramount, a precursor to attaining a flag rank. He is recorded as being a squadron commander in 1786 but this high rank was to be problematic as the French Revolution began.

Jean-Baptiste's high social and naval status led to him being the head of a military tribunal, trying a case of alleged mutiny against a much-disliked captain. Despite the involvement of 'behind the scenes politics' and the emerging revolutionary attitudes of the people, Jean-Baptiste found the accused captain not guilty. At some point after this he went to London to escape the revolution. He was a wealthy and powerful aristocrat, being among the 42 richest citizens who were ordered to surrender a quarter of their income to the cause in 1792.

The story of Jean-Baptiste concludes in 1802 when, as an old man, he decided to return to France. Whether this was because he missed his native home or the French government had relaxed the rules, as by now they had realised most of their experienced naval officers had been guillotined, to their cost in lost battles, is not known. Sadly he died on his way home and was buried in St Michael's churchyard. His headstone bears the family coat of arms surrounded by a rope and the emblem of the Order of St Louis.

Bibliography

Books

Abbey, A., *The Sittingbourne Anomaly* (2006)

Ashbee, P., *Kent in Prehistoric Times* (2005)

Bellingham, Dr P., *Sittingbourne and Milton* (1996)

Clancy, J., *Sittingbourne and Milton Regis Past and Present* (1999)

Clancy, J., *The Story of Sittingbourne and Milton Regis* (2002)

Davis, R.H.C. and Chibnall, M., *The Gesta Guillelmi of William of Poitiers* (1998)

Deakin, W.H., *Sittingbourne and Milton Regis: A Conservation Study* (1974)

Diack, M., *A Bronze Age Settlement at Kemsley, near Sittingbourne, Kent* (2006)

Feakes, L., *Woodstock: An Archaeological Mystery* (2001)

Glover, J., *The Place Names of Kent* (1982)

Griffin, R., *The Lepers' Hospital at Swainestrey* (1921)

Historical Research Group of Sittingbourne (ed. Clancy, J.), *The Story of Brenchley House* (2006)

Homan, R., *The Victorian Churches of Kent* (1984)

Ireland, W.H., *A New and Complete History of the County of Kent,* reprint (1828)

Jessup, F.W., *Kent History Illustrated* (1966)

Lawson, T. and Killingray, D., *An Historical Atlas of Kent* (2004)

MacDougall, P., *Chatham Past* (1999)

Sattin, D., *Barge Building on the Kentish Swale* (1980)

Scott Robertson, W.A., *Sittingbourne and the Names of Lands and Houses In or Near It: Their Origin and History,* reprint (1879)

Twist, S., *Stock Bricks of Swale* (1984)

Articles

Parfitt, K., 'Where Was The Broken Tower?', *Kent Archaeological Review*, No.156 (2004)

Ward, A., 'A Brief Note on the Broken Tower', *Kent Archaeological Review*, No.157 (2004)

Index

References in bold refer to pages on which there are illustrations.